Sew Me, Love Me

Best Stuffed Friends to Make

Hsiu-Lan Kuei

First published in the United States by:

Interweave Press LLC
201 East Fourth Street
Loveland, CO 80537-5655 USA
interweavestore.com

Printed in China

Library of Congress Cataloging-in-Publication Data

Kuei, Hsiu-Lan.
 Sew me, love me : best stuffed friends to make / Hsiu-Lan Kuei.
    p. cm.
 Includes index.
 ISBN 978-1-59668-182-8 (pbk.)
 1. Soft toy making. 2. Stuffed animals (Toys) I. Title.
 TT174.3.K84 2009
 745.592'4--dc22
                          2009013741

10 9 8 7 6 5 4 3 2 1

Introduction

A doll-making hobby is a wonderful skill to cultivate in your free time. In winter, sitting near a window, bathed in the warm sun, sewing a fun new doll by hand is a perfect way to pass the time. With my dog resting his head on my lap and watching the doll take shape, I feel warmth and happiness filling the air.

I hope this book inspires you to create your own dolls and share the same happiness I feel when sewing by hand.

The Doll Family

The more you sew, the more that dolls will become part of your life. I have an ever-growing number of dolls at home and they have become one big (stuffed!) family. I find myself thinking often of the new clothes I can make for them, or deciding who I should take on my next trip.

Although my handmade dolls may not look as polished as store-bought dolls, I feel so proud when I turn recycled fabric into these simple, adorable dolls. Children especially seem to cherish these homemade dolls…and I hope they are learning something about recycling through them, too.

Pick me! Me!

Part 1

How to Make Friends:
Doll Making with Recycled Materials

Before I started making dolls, I was like everyone else: I'd throw away my old clothes or donate them to charity. Doll making inspired me to breathe new life into all these old items of clothing! It's such a treat to discover new, unexpected uses for cloth scraps. Orphaned socks, shrunken sweaters, faded cloth, dated accessories, and worn-out cushions—you name it, it can be used in doll making.

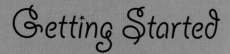

Getting Started

We can always find old clothes tucked in the bottom of drawers and at the back of the closet. Stray socks, old sweaters, ill-fitting tops—it never ends! (Make sure they're clean!)

Fabrics

Everyone's wardrobe contains a variety of fabrics. Any and all of these materials can be used to make dolls. Sewing from outgrown children's clothes is a great way to incorporate a piece of a favorite dress or T-shirt into a doll. The doll itself becomes a memento or a time capsule! Bed sheets, towels, T-shirts, socks, shirts, and jeans offer even more cotton fabric choices.

When planning the construction of the doll's body, consider the elasticity of the fabric. If the fabric has a bit of stretch, you can stuff the doll's figure to give it a unique shape. Socks and other knits are perfect for making the body.

Using the right part of an item of clothing is also key to great doll making. The front-center point of a V-neck top can easily turn into a mini V-neck top for your doll. Some simple stitches will turn a sleeve into a turtleneck sweater. The only limit is your imagination!

I like to curl up in Daddy's shirt.

Children's clothes are great for doll making. They are often more colorful than their adult versions, so they can be turned into doll clothes easily. They are also fun to chew on.

Faded and well-loved clothes have a soft, natural, even vintage look. On a doll you can feel the softness of the worn fabric.

Hey Baby . . .

Prairie Pup's sweater is made from a striped sock.

The dolls' bodies and tops are sewn from recycled knit fabric.

A sleeve from a ribbed sweater was transformed into a sweater for Bob.

11

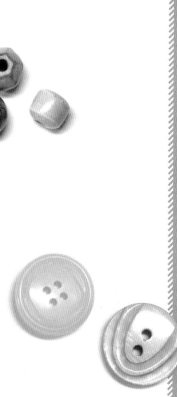

Buttons and Beads

Once I started making dolls, I began to snip off all the buttons from my old clothes before discarding them or putting them in the rag pile. You never know what kind of button will be perfect for a future doll! Beads can be harvested and saved from outdated accessories or dismantled jewelry. You can always go to a craft or bead store if you need to find a particular shape or color.

Buttons and beads are used as eyes and noses for the dolls. Clusters or stacks of beads and buttons can become decorative pieces or other accessories on the doll.

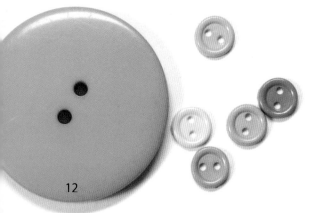

12

The flat two- or four-hole button secures a limb to the body, such as at the shoulder—wherever movement is needed.

Comb through your stash of buttons and beads to find the best pieces for your doll!

This flesh-tone button is a perfect pig snout! Oink!

I see stars!

A star-shaped bead stacked atop the pearly button makes the frog's eyes sparkle.

13

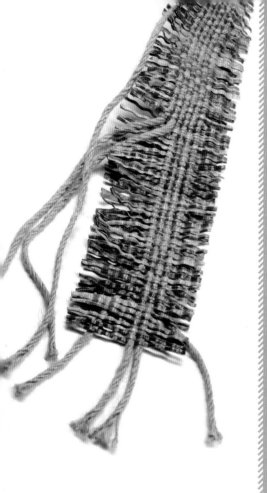

Cords, Strings, and Ribbons

Cords, strings, and ribbons play many roles in doll making. They can be turned into hair, tails, or even a necktie for a dapper, well-dressed doll! Craft wire can be used as the armature (skeleton) for dolls you'd like to bend and twist into shape.

Don't forget to salvage shoelaces from old sneakers and shoes. Yarn raveled from a worn-out sweater makes "naturally" curly hair for your doll. Ribbons from unwrapped gifts, rope from shopping bag handles, and thread from frayed woven fabric can all be used in doll making. Those unique cords, strings, and ribbons that can't be found at home can be found in a craft or hardware store—be creative!

All types of cords, ropes, wires, and ribbons can be used in doll making!

This wiggly worm is made from craft wire! See how my shape can be changed?

This beautiful curly hair is the yarn from a raveled sweater.

15

Stuffing

Recycling the stuffing from worn-out cushions and pillows is an excellent source of doll-making material. The fabric from the cushions and pillows is great for clothing, too.

Lofty polyester fill is easy to manipulate into different body shapes. Try removing the stuffing from children's worn stuffed animals. Yarn and fabric scraps from the animals can be used as stuffing, too (or even repurposed into other doll parts).

Help! I've fallen and I can't get up!

A chopstick can help fill long, narrow limbs with stuffing.

Leftover yarn and fabric scraps can come in handy as stuffing.

Polyester or cotton fill is typically used in commercial stuffed dolls.

Plastic beads or beans add weight to a doll's body and limbs.

Tools and Supplies

Basic Doll-Making Tools

With the right tools, sewing dolls can be simple and yield great results. However, even with just a pair of scissors and a needle and thread, you can get started with doll making.

All the tools illustrated here can be found at most department stores or craft stores. A sewing machine will make sewing a lot faster but it is not necessary. You may find that sewing dolls by hand gives them a cozy, handmade feel.

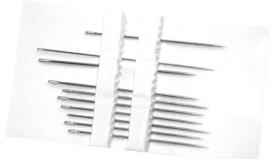

Hand-sewing needles

Threads in different colors

Pencils (for pattern tracing)

Tape measure

Ruler

Tailor's chalk

Thread snips

Erasable fabric pen

Seam ripper

Awl or needle tool

Scissors (for paper)

Fabric scissors

Quilting pins

Don't be dull. *Using one pair of scissors for paper and another pair for fabric will prolong the sharpness of the blades.*

Basic Hand Stitches

Several basic hand stitches are used in doll making. Once you know these basic stitches, you will be able to determine which stitches are best for certain steps and patterns. Begin all stitch techniques with a hand-sewing needle threaded with 18" (45 cm) of thread. Tie a knot in the end of the thread before taking the first stitch, or tie a knot with your first stitch into the fabric.

Stitch length: ⅛" (3 mm)

Running Stitch This stitch is used mostly for seams and for decorative edging. Try a running stitch when adding facial expressions or details. Insert the needle in and out of the fabric several times (1–5) , then pull the thread through the fabric. Keep the stitches and the spaces between them short and even.

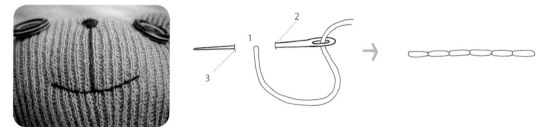

Backstitch This is a dense stitch that works best on stretchy fabric, such as socks and knits. Pull the needle and thread to the front of the fabric (1). Insert the needle ¹⁄₁₆" to ⅛" (1.6 to 3 mm) behind where the thread exited the fabric (2). Then bring the needle out through the fabric the same distance away from that point (3). Repeat.

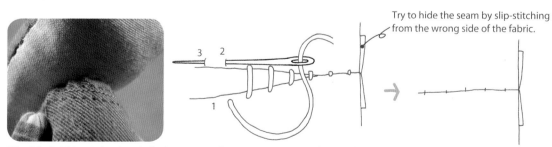

Try to hide the seam by slip-stitching from the wrong side of the fabric.

Slip Stitch This stitch is handy for hemming, closing open seams (after stuffing, for example), and joining doll parts. Simple, regular ladder-like stitches are made to join two fabric edges.

 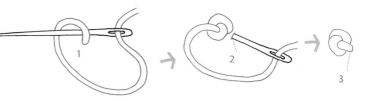

French Knot These stitches add raised details and texture. French knots are ideal for highlighting a doll's whiskers. Pull the needle and thread to the front of the fabric. Form a small loop, insert the needle through the loop (1). Insert needle right next to (1) to secure knot (2). Pull the thread taut (3).

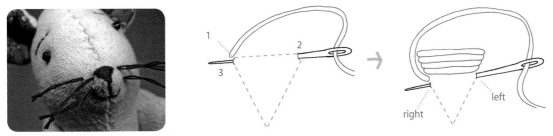

Chain Stitch Each stitch is "chained" to the previous one (as shown above). This stitch is often used for the mouth, eyebrows, or other facial details for the dolls. Pull needle through (1) and insert needle beside 1 (2). Poke needle through at (3), loop thread around needle. Pull taut. Repeat for each stitch.

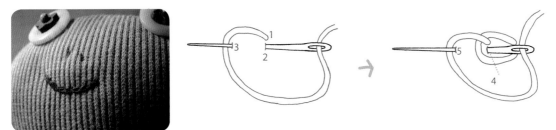

Satin Stitch The satin stitch is used to fill shapes on the surface of fabric, such as noses or lips. Draw the shape lightly on the fabric with chalk or pencil. Lay the first stitch along one edge (1–2), then lay several more stitches close together (but not overlapping) the length of the shape (3). The stitches should all be equally taut to create a flat, satin-like texture.

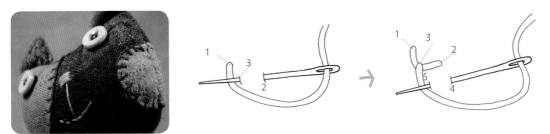

Overcast (or Blanket) Stitch This stitch is used for finishing seams and decorative edges. It can also be used for appliqué. Form a series of close, evenly spaced stitches by passing the thread over and around the fabric edge (as shown above).

Basic Techniques for Doll Making

Playing with Stuffing

Most dolls are made from several separate stuffed pieces, usually at least the head and the nose (or snout).

How to Make a Stuffed Nose

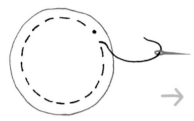 →  →

Cut a small circle from the doll body (or nose) fabric. With running stitches, sew around the edge of the circle.

Place stuffing on the wrong side of the circle, then pull the thread to form a pouch. Fill the pouch with more stuffing as needed.

Cinch the pouch closed and make a knot in the thread. You now have a little ball to use as a nose.

You can change the size of the nose or muzzle by starting with a larger fabric circle.

★ How to Create Nostrils

Insert the needle into the nostril area from one side. Make a large knot. Pull the needle through from the other side of the nose. Pull the thread taut and make another large knot. The taut thread will give the impression of nostrils.

Attaching the Arms: The Axle Method

The method below creates joints that allow the limbs to move. (This is referred to in this book as the axle method.) The secret is that thread and buttons are formed into an axle-like structure. The buttons also add a decorative element to the doll's design.

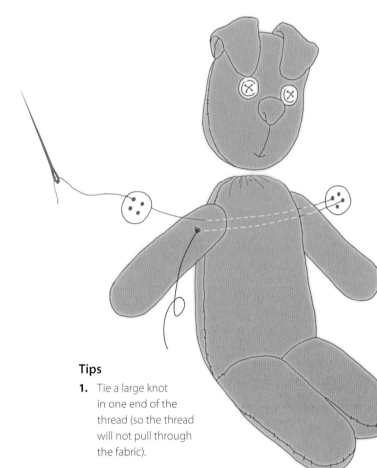

Tips

1. Tie a large knot in one end of the thread (so the thread will not pull through the fabric).

2. Place the knot so it will be hidden beneath the button.

Instructions

1. Snip a length of thread that is four times the width of the doll's shoulders. Thread a needle and make a large knot in the end.

2. Insert the needle through the outside of one arm, push the needle and thread through the entire body, and pull the needle out at the outside of the other arm. Slip one button onto the needle and take a diagonal stitch across to a second hole, anchoring the button.

3. Pull the needle through the body and out again where you began in step 2. Attach the second button in the same manner. Stitch back and forth through the buttons and the body until both buttons are secured to the sides.

4. The thread should be taut and the buttons should be fastened tightly on each side. Hide the last stitch and knot underneath one of the arms.

Part 2
The Projects: Dolls You Can Make by Hand

We are all one of a kind. We each have different tastes, different habits, and different fashion sense. This universal uniqueness is the heart and soul of our lives.

You do not need to follow my pattern, my fabric choices, or my style. Use, reuse, and experiment with anything you can find for creating your very own doll. Use these projects as a foundation for your new knowledge and experiences in doll making. Ideally you will find your own patterns and style and conjure up dolls that uniquely express *you*.

Discovering your own tricks and finding new materials from your closet will add to the fun of doll making. Not only will you have the satisfaction of making your own doll but you will also enjoy clever, handmade, and homespun recycling.

Froggy Friends

These frogs have a simple pattern construction and bold, expressive details, and are a great first doll-making project! Try to find a stretchy fabric for the body that can be shaped and molded easily. The simplicity of the patterns is ideal for experimenting with color, unique beads and buttons, and colored or textured thread.

Step by Step

MATERIALS

✓ Green stretchy fabric
  (for the body)
✓ Red fabric (for the bandana)
✓ 2 large green buttons and
  2 small yellow buttons
  (for the eyes)
✓ Yellow and green thread
✓ Stuffing

★ Patterns: pages 130–131

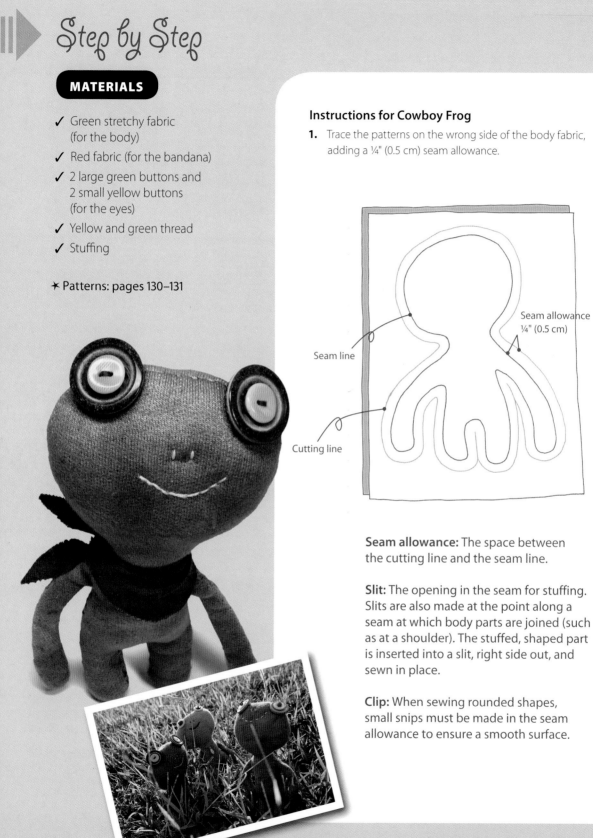

Instructions for Cowboy Frog

1. Trace the patterns on the wrong side of the body fabric, adding a ¼" (0.5 cm) seam allowance.

Seam allowance ¼" (0.5 cm)

Seam line

Cutting line

Seam allowance: The space between the cutting line and the seam line.

Slit: The opening in the seam for stuffing. Slits are also made at the point along a seam at which body parts are joined (such as at a shoulder). The stuffed, shaped part is inserted into a slit, right side out, and sewn in place.

Clip: When sewing rounded shapes, small snips must be made in the seam allowance to ensure a smooth surface.

2. With a running stitch, sew along the seam line. Be sure to leave a 1" (2 cm) slit.

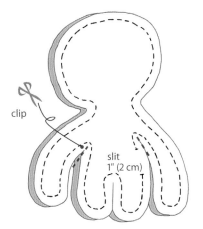

clip

slit
1" (2 cm)

3. Turn the doll right side out through the slit. Fill the doll with stuffing. Use a dowel or wire to push the stuffing into the corners. With a slip stitch, sew the slit closed.

Do not stuff the upper half of the arms completely so they can move freely.

4. With yellow thread, sew the nose and mouth of the frog. Use running stitches for the nostrils and backstitches for the mouth. With green thread, sew the eyes. Stack a small yellow button on top of a larger green button for each eye. Sew one button stack to each side of the forehead.

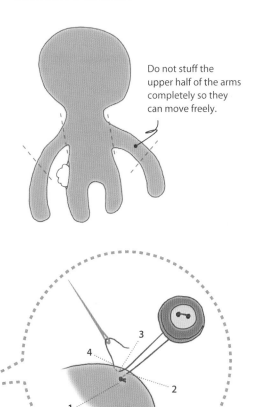

The buttons will hide the knot.

When you start to sew the eyes, be sure the buttons are placed so they will fully hide the knots!

Creating Facial Expressions

Sewing expressive facial details on your dolls is the most challenging as well as the most dynamic part of doll making. A doll's facial features give it life and show its true character. During the process of constructing a doll, you need to communicate with it to unearth its hidden personality…and quirks.

*Hand stitching shows more variation between stitches. While machine stitching is smooth and uniform, a crafter's handwork makes each doll unique.

I'm taller!

Smooth machine-sewn stitches

Hand-sewn slip stitches

FACIAL EXPRESSIONS

HAPPY
Eyes: Use buttons with two holes. Sewing horizontal stitches across the holes will create a "smiley" effect.

Mouth: Back stitches sewn in a medium-size smile make a happy face.

SILLY
Eyes: Combine a few different buttons and beads for the eye to give the frog a quirky expression.

Mouth: Broad running stitches shaping a large mouth create an exaggerated expression.

SWEET
Eyes: Flower-shaped buttons as the pupils makes the frog look cute and charming.

Mouth: Split running stitches and a shorter curve creates a more feminine mouth.

ACCESSORIES

BANDANA

Cut a long, wide triangle from red jersey, about 9¾" (17 cm) long and 2½"(6 cm) wide. Tie the bandana around the frog's neck for instant cowboy style.

NECKLACE

Shorten the cord of a simple seashell necklace so it fits the frog's neck.

Spotlight

THE EYES HAVE IT

The key to creating unique facial expressions for your dolls is experimenting with a variety of buttons and beads in many combinations.

When choosing buttons and beads, first consider the size of the doll's face and determine the size of the eyes. Then you can select the right color(s) and material(s), and plan the stitches for sewing all the elements together. Remember, the more buttons, beads, and other miscellaneous hardware you've harvested from old clothes and accessories, the greater range of expressions you can create for a doll!

Every crafter has her own vision for how a doll should look. Use your own intuition and imagination to create unique characters. With practice you will not only master the actual doll-making techniques but also the personality-shaping techniques for making faces with buttons and stitches.

The Right Stitch for the Right Button

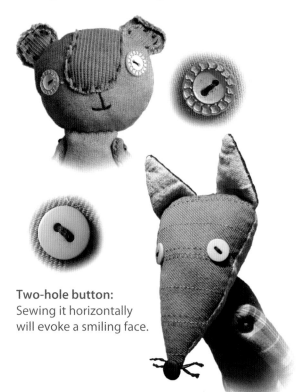

Two-hole button: Sewing it horizontally will evoke a smiling face.

Zany two-button: Stack a small black two-hole button on a white button and thread it through only one of the white button's holes. This alignment creates a zany, loopy look in the eyes.

BUTTON AND BEAD COMBINATIONS

Different smaller buttons on the same base button

Four-hole button: Sewing the button in an X shape (stitching across the diagonal) may soften your doll's expression, or it may make it look cross-eyed (depending on the doll's personality).

Sewing in a square shape (stitching one side at a time) will make the pupil appear full and large.

Monochromatic color scheme

Consider sewing eyelashes around the eyes with simple stitches—the length and placement of the lashes can enhance your doll's expression.

Contrasting color scheme

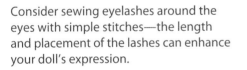

Small bead on a button

Multiple layers of beads and buttons

It's raining cats and socks!

Mr. Stripey the Cat

Socks are one of my favorite materials for doll making. A whole sock makes a great doll body, or parts of the sock can be used as a colorful decorative piece. Because of the variety of colors, patterns, and materials socks are available in, the styles of sock dolls you can make are infinite!

Bedtime Bear, on page 40, is made from a pair of gray ribbed socks. This doll is perfect for a colorful striped sock.

Step by Step

MATERIALS

- ✓ 1 striped sock
- ✓ 2 large beads and two small beads (for the eyes)
- ✓ 1 black button (for the nose)
- ✓ Yellow thread
- ✓ Stuffing

Instructions for Mr. Stripey the Cat

1. Considering the placement and size of the stripes, mark the cutting lines (and seam allowances) for the doll parts with an erasable marking pen. Cut out all parts.

   ✶ You do not need to leave a seam allowance for the inner and outer part of the ears.

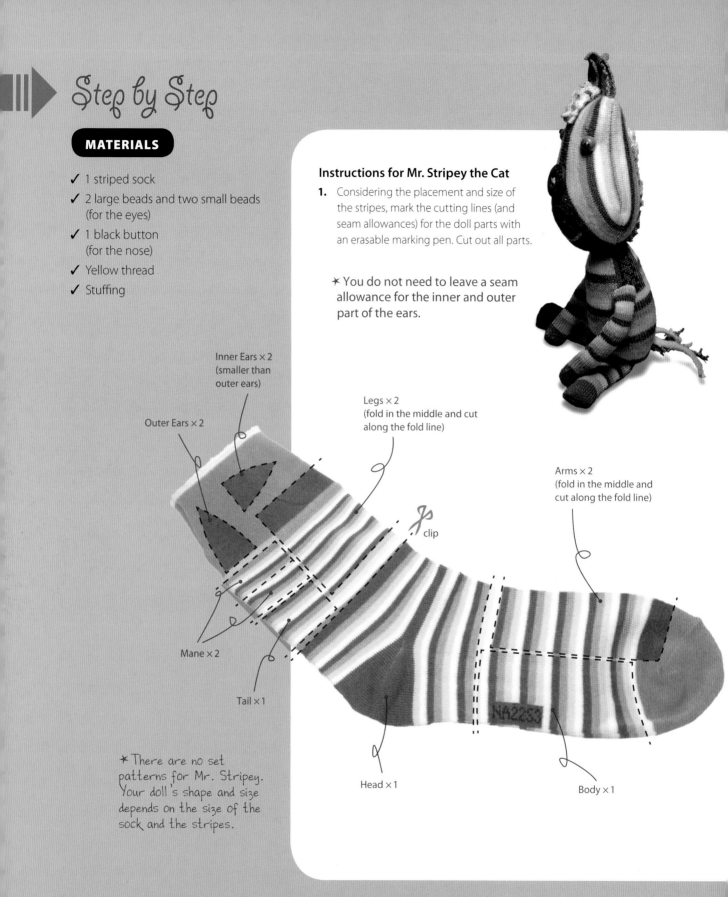

Inner Ears × 2 (smaller than outer ears)

Outer Ears × 2

Legs × 2 (fold in the middle and cut along the fold line)

Arms × 2 (fold in the middle and cut along the fold line)

clip

Mane × 2

Tail × 1

Head × 1

Body × 1

✶ There are no set patterns for Mr. Stripey. Your doll's shape and size depends on the size of the sock and the stripes.

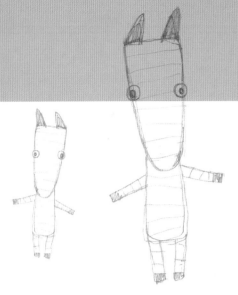

3. Sandwich the two finished ears along the open seam at the top of the head, aligning the base of the ears with the top of the head. The wrong sides of the fabric for the head should face out. With a backstitch, sew along the dotted line (see below). Make sure to leave about a 1" (2 cm) slit on the side of the head. Turn the head right side out and fill with stuffing.

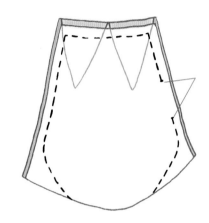

2. To create the ears: Layer one piece of the inner ear and one piece of the outer ear. With a running stitch and yellow thread, sew along the dotted line (see illustration).

4. Stack a small bead on top of a larger bead for each eye. Sew both eyes in place. Sew the black button where the nose should be. With yellow thread and a split running stitch, sew the mouth.

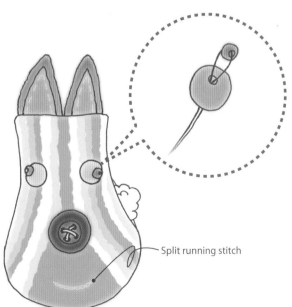

Split running stitch

5. Fold the body fabric in half vertically and sew along the dotted line (see illustration). Turn the body right side out and fill with stuffing. Attach the head to the body with slip stitches.

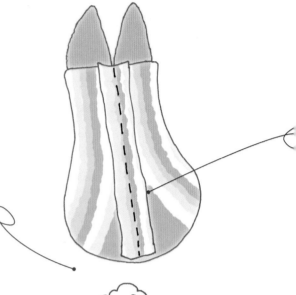

6. Fold each piece of arm fabric in half vertically and sew along the dotted line (see illustration). Turn each arm right side out and fill with stuffing. Attach the arms to the body with slip stitches.

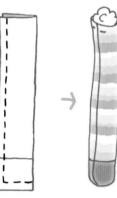

7. Repeat step 6 for both pieces of leg fabric.

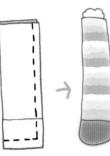

8. Layer the two pieces of mane fabric. With running stitches, sew the mane between the ears, from the forehead to back of the head. Snip the fabric along the edges to create fringe, leaving ¼" (0.5 cm) between each cut. Do not cut through the mane's stitches.

Layer two pieces of mane fabric before sewing, then cut the fabric finely on the edges.

9. Roll the tail fabric tightly. Secure one end with a few stitches. Cut the roll lengthwise into several thin strips with ¼" (0.5 cm) between each cut. Sew the tail to the back of the body with slip stitches.

Be sure one side of the tail is secured with stitches before cutting!

Bedtime Bear

This bear is my first handmade doll. He does not have splashy colors, and his face is simple and serious. (You may think he even looks a little bit sad!) Even his stitches are somewhat messy. Even though I've made many more dolls since this one, I still cherish him the most.

Step by Step

MATERIALS

✓ 1 pair of gray ribbed socks (for all body parts)

✓ 2 large black buttons (for the shoulders)

✓ 2 brown buttons (for the eyes)

✓ Black thread (for the nose, eyes, and eyebrows)

✓ Brown thread (for the mouth and whiskers)

✓ Stuffing

★ Patterns: pages 132-133

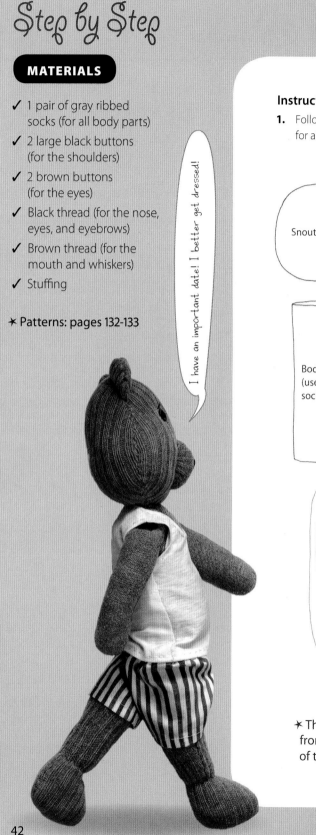

I have an important date! I better get dressed!

Instructions for Bedtime Bear

1. Follow the diagram. With an erasable pen mark the cutting lines for all body parts. Cut out along the lines.

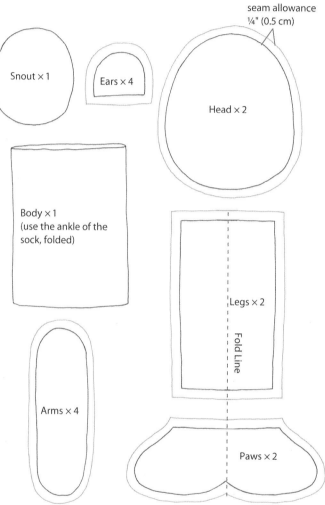

seam allowance ¼" (0.5 cm)

Snout × 1

Ears × 4

Head × 2

Body × 1 (use the ankle of the sock, folded)

Legs × 2

Fold Line

Arms × 4

Paws × 2

★ The patterns allow you to make the Sock Teddy Bear from any fabric you choose. Enlarge or reduce the size of the patterns, depending on the size of your socks.

*Cutting Guide

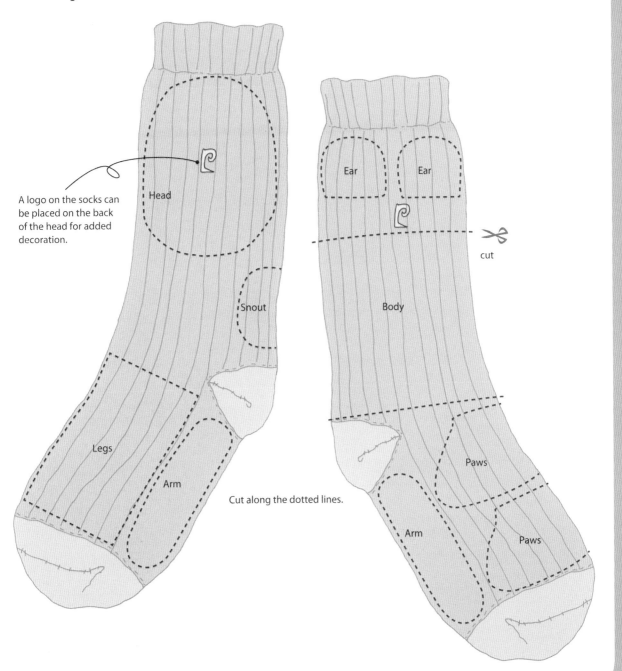

A logo on the socks can be placed on the back of the head for added decoration.

Head

Ear　Ear

Snout

Body

Legs

Arm

Cut along the dotted lines.

Paws

Arm

Paws

cut

2. Sew two ear pieces together along the curved edge (see illustration), right sides facing. Leave a seam allowance of about ¼" (0.5 cm). Turn the ears right side out through the slit.

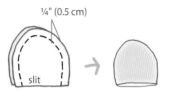

¼" (0.5 cm)

slit

3. Sandwich the finished ears between the head pieces. The bottom edge of the ears should align with the top edge of the head. Make sure the right sides of the head pieces face each other. With a running stitch, sew the head pieces together (see illustration). Turn the head right side out through the slit. Fill the head with stuffing and sew the slit closed with slip stitches.

4. With erasable pen, outline the facial features of the bear.

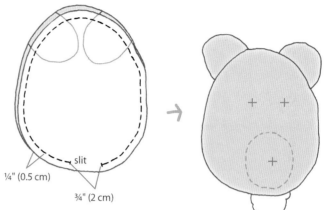

slit

¼" (0.5 cm)

¾" (2 cm)

5. Create the snout: see page 22 for complete instructions. It is sewn separately, then stitched in place on the head. With a satin stitch and black thread, create the nostril. Sew the whiskers, mouth, eyes, and eyebrows.

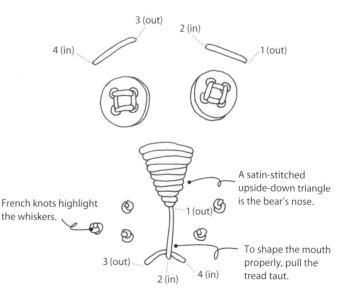

3 (out)

2 (in)

4 (in)

1 (out)

French knots highlight the whiskers.

A satin-stitched upside-down triangle is the bear's nose.

1 (out)

To shape the mouth properly, pull the tread taut.

3 (out)

2 (in)

4 (in)

✷ Refer to page 22 for instructions on creating a snout.

6. Fold the leg and paw pieces in half vertically. With running stitches, sew along the dotted line (see illustration).

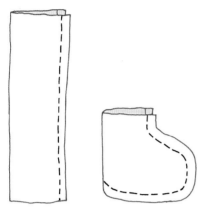

8. Sandwich both legs between the body pieces (see illustration), with right sides of body fabric together. Sew the legs to the body with a running stitch.

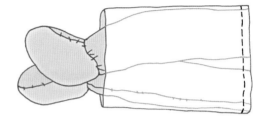

9. Turn the body right side out and fill with stuffing. Sew a running stitch around the neck opening and pull the stitches taut to close the neck.

7. Turn the legs and paws right side out. Attach the paws to the legs with slip stitches, then fill with stuffing.

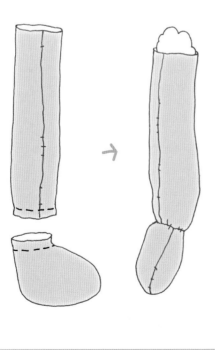

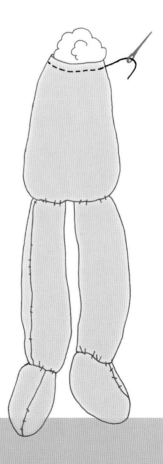

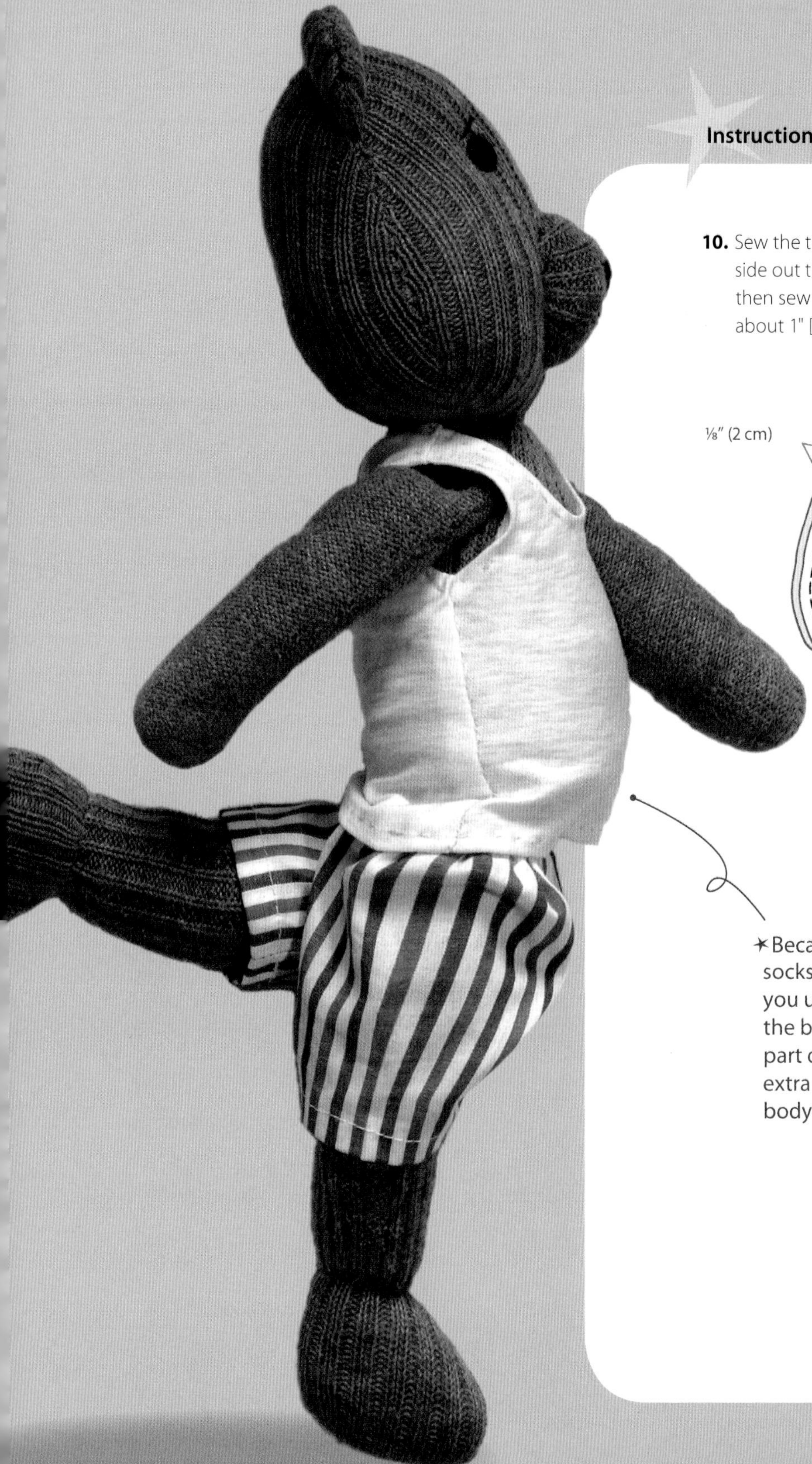

10. Sew the two arm pieces together, then turn right
side out through the slit. Stuff the arm via the slit,
then sew the openings closed. (The slit should be
about 1" [2 cm].)

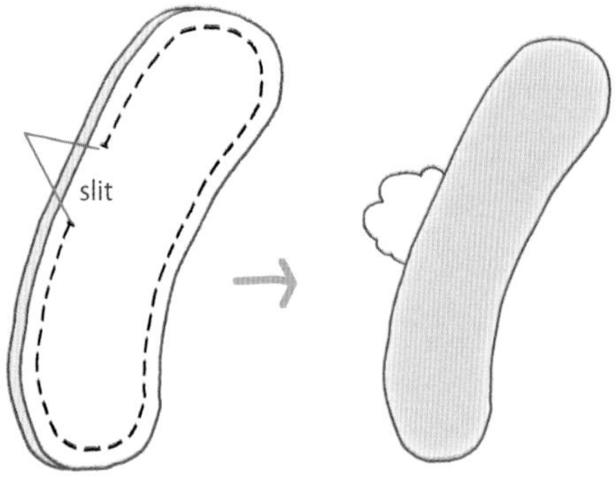

⅛" (2 cm)

slit

★ Because of the elasticity of the
socks, the amount of stuffing
you use will affect the shape of
the bear. Do not overfill every
part of the body, but try using
extra filling in the bear's lower
body to give it a fat tummy.

11. Attach the head to the body with slip stitches. To attach the arms to the body, use the Axle Method illustrated on page 23.

illustrated on page 23.

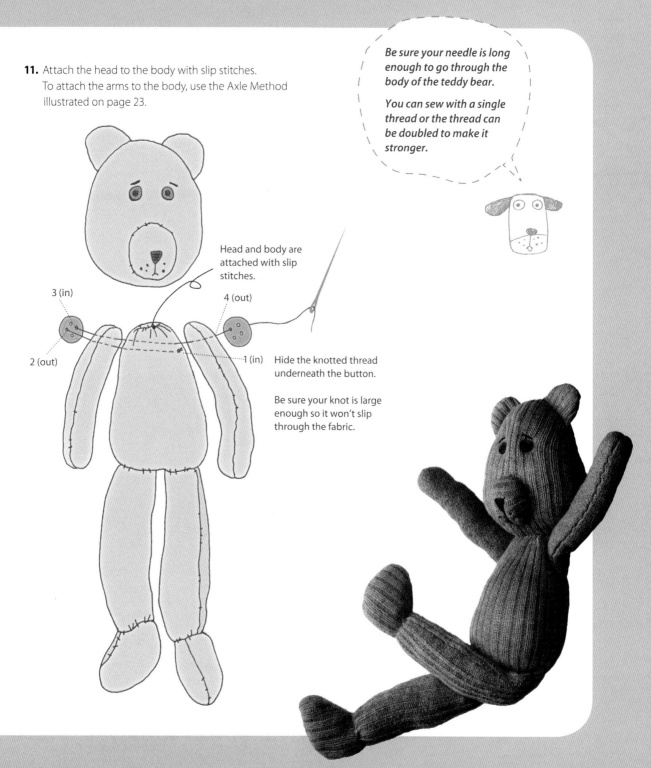

Be sure your needle is long enough to go through the body of the teddy bear.

You can sew with a single thread or the thread can be doubled to make it stronger.

Head and body are attached with slip stitches.

3 (in)

4 (out)

2 (out)

1 (in)

Hide the knotted thread underneath the button.

Be sure your knot is large enough so it won't slip through the fabric.

Shirt

MATERIALS

✓ White fabric
✓ White thread

★ Pattern: page 133

Instructions

1. Trace the patterns onto your fabric, leaving a seam allowance (as indicated). Cut out the patterns.

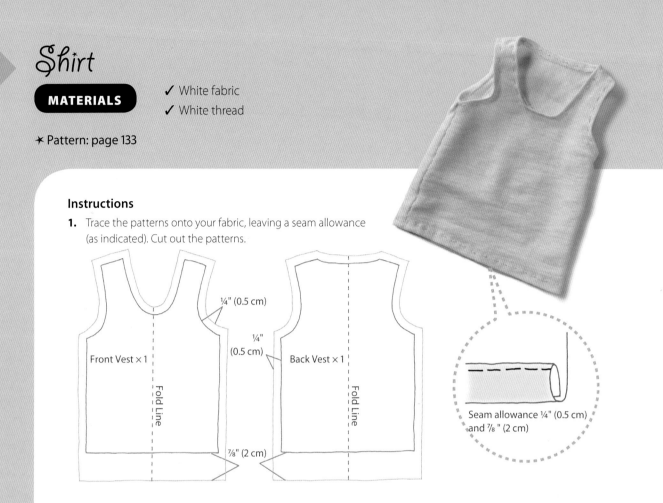

¼" (0.5 cm)

¼" (0.5 cm)

Front Vest × 1

Fold Line

Back Vest × 1

Fold Line

⅞" (2 cm)

Seam allowance ¼" (0.5 cm) and ⅞ " (2 cm)

2. With right sides of the shirt facing, sew the shoulders and main body parts together.

3. Around the neckline, arm openings, and bottom edge, turn up the seam allowances and sew the hem.

4. To hide the rough edge on the bottom edge, you need to fold the hem three times (as shown in the illustration).

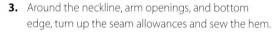

3rd

2nd

1st

★**Triple-folded hem:**
Determine the width of the hem (usually about ⅜" [1 cm]). Working from the wrong side, fold the hem three times. With a running stitch, stitch it in place.

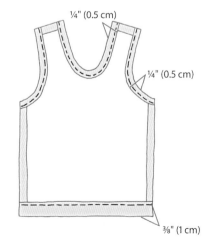

¼" (0.5 cm)

¼" (0.5 cm)

⅜" (1 cm)

Shorts

MATERIALS

★ Patterns: page 133

✓ Striped cotton fabric
✓ Elastic (for the waistband) 3¼" (8 cm) long
✓ White thread

Instructions

1. Trace the pattern on the wrong side of the fabric, leaving a small seam allowance on all sides.

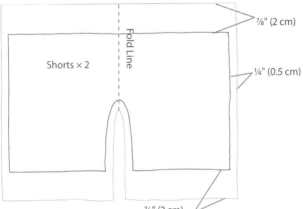

Fold Line

Shorts × 2

⅞" (2 cm)

¼" (0.5 cm)

⅞" (2 cm)

2. From the wrong side of the fabric, sew the outer and inner thigh seams with a running stitch.

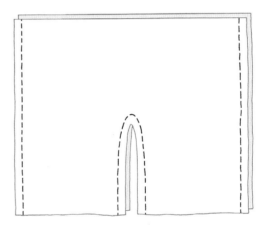

3. Create a hem at the waistband and the cuffs. Fold the hem three times before sewing (as with the vest). Leave ⅜" (1 cm) wide channel for the waistband casing. Feed the elastic through the casing and stitch the elastic ends together firmly.

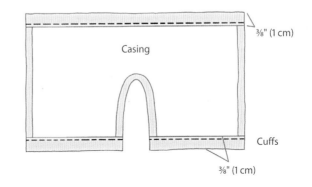

Casing

⅜" (1 cm)

Cuffs

⅜" (1 cm)

49

Scrappy Lion

Like many crafters and sewers, I have a lot of fabric scraps left over from various sewing projects. All together, they take the shape of a lion's mane!

As a beginner doll maker, I tried to make my dolls looks as realistic as possible, with perfectly symmetrical bodies and perfectly expressive features. Later, as my skills developed, I grew more adventurous and playful, and I became more free-form with my doll making. With his messy mane and asymmetrical body, my Scrappy Lion represents creative freedom in doll making!

Step by Step

MATERIALS

- ✓ Purple fabric with some stretch (for the body)
- ✓ Pink fabric (for the nose and mouth)
- ✓ Assorted fabric scraps (for the mane)
- ✓ 2 small dark brown beads (for the pupils)
- ✓ 2 flat blue beads (for the irises)
- ✓ 2 large light brown buttons (for the eyes)
- ✓ 2 large brown beads (for the shoulders)
- ✓ Dark brown thread (for the mouth and whiskers)
- ✓ White thread
- ✓ Stuffing

★ Patterns: page 134

Rowr!

Instructions for Scrappy Lion

1. Trace the template on the fabric, leaving a ¼" (0.5 cm) seam allowance.

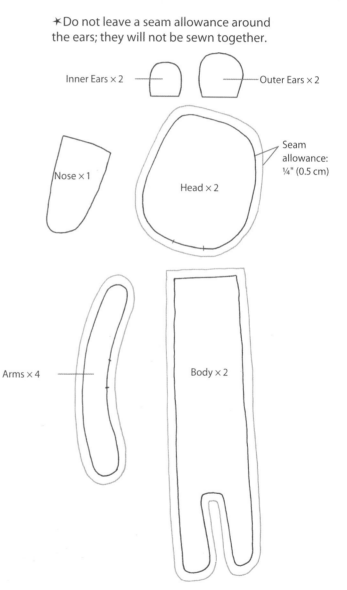

★Do not leave a seam allowance around the ears; they will not be sewn together.

Inner Ears × 2

Outer Ears × 2

Nose × 1

Head × 2

Seam allowance: ¼" (0.5 cm)

Arms × 4

Body × 2

2. Layer the nose piece on one head piece, aligning the edges. Sew them together, leaving the top of the nose open. Stuff the nose, then sew the opening closed.

✴ The nose needs just a small amount of stuffing.

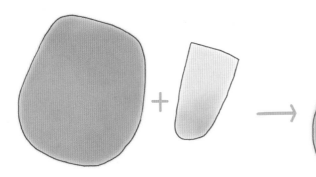

3. Layer the inner ear pieces over the outer ear pieces, aligning the bottom edges, and sew them together. Sandwich the ears between the head pieces, aligning the bottom of the ears with the outside head edge. Make sure the head pieces are placed wrong side out. Sew around the head, leaving a slit at the bottom that measures about ⅞" (2 cm) long (for stuffing).

4. Turn the head right side out so the face faces out. Stack the three beads to create the eyes, using the smallest beads as the pupils. Sew eyes to the face. With a backstitch, outline the mouth, then create whiskers with French knots.

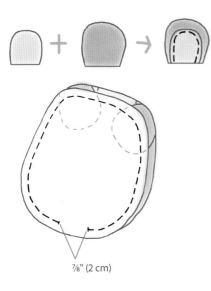

⅞" (2 cm)

✴ Fill the head with stuffing through the neck slit. With a slip stitch, sew the slit closed.

Sewing the Doll's Body

Most of my dolls are human-shaped in that they have arms and legs and "walk" upright. Even if you are making a stuffed animal, you can exaggerate their features and give them cartoon-like arms or legs. This will liven up their personalities!

Another way to add to the character of the doll is with the tail. Stretch your imagination and you can create totally unique-shaped tails for your beloved doll pets.

5. With right sides facing, align two arm pieces. Sew them together, leaving a ⅞" (2 cm) slit for stuffing. Repeat with two other arm pieces. Turn arms right side out.

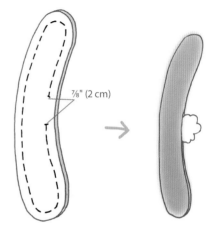

⅞" (2 cm)

6. With right sides facing, align the body pieces. Sew them together, leaving a small opening at the neck for stuffing. Turn the body right side out.

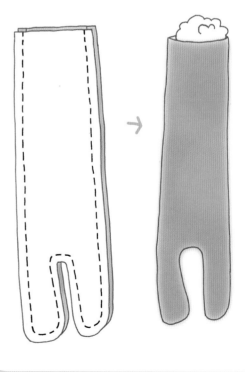

7. With a slip stitch, sew the head, body, and arms together. Cut a strip of fabric about ½" × 1½" (1.5 × 4 cm) long for the lion's tail. Sew one end of the tail to the body, and sew colorful fabric scraps to the end of the tail.

8. Sew multicolored (and multi-sized) fabric scraps in a ring around the head (sewing into the seam, if desired) to create the mane.

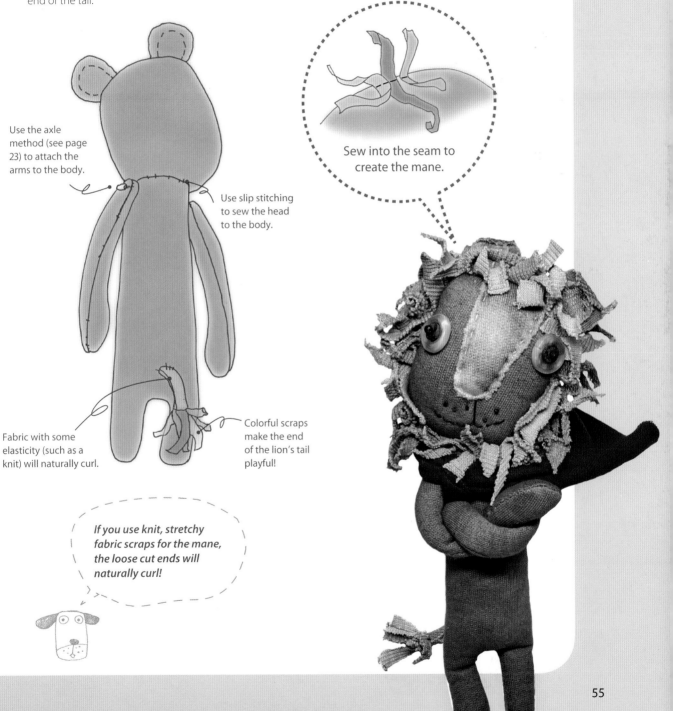

Use the axle method (see page 23) to attach the arms to the body.

Use slip stitching to sew the head to the body.

Sew into the seam to create the mane.

Fabric with some elasticity (such as a knit) will naturally curl.

Colorful scraps make the end of the lion's tail playful!

If you use knit, stretchy fabric scraps for the mane, the loose cut ends will naturally curl!

55

Variation:

Styling Hair for Your Dolls

Being your doll's hair stylist is another way to express your doll's personality. Twist, tie, and shape any kind of thread, yarn, hemp, or even strips of fabric to dress up your dolls. Just stitch the hair material to the head and vary the color, length, and texture.

To find novel hair materials, comb through your old sweaters, towels, sheets, and discarded clothing. Just about anything can be turned into hair!

String from frayed woven fabric can be used for the hair.

Instructions for hair

1. Determine the length of the doll's hair. Make several equal-sized loops of yarn, string, or cord. How thick you'd like the hair determines the number of loops you make.

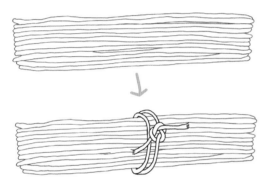

Wrap a separate strand of yarn or string around the middle of the hair and tie a tight knot.

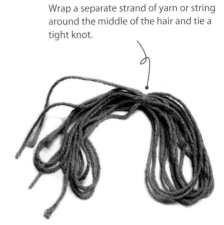

2. Cut through the loops on both ends of the hair.

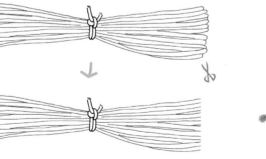

3. Starting from the forehead and with a backstitch, sew the hair to the doll's head. Trim the hair to shape it to your style.

Cool, daddy-o . . .

Beatnik Bob

Many parts of discarded clothing—necklines, hems, and
more—can be repurposed for doll making. With a few
snips and stitches, a sleeve from a ribbed knit sweater
becomes the perfect turtleneck for Beatnik Bear.
A swatch of fabric from an old pair of corduroys was sewn
into pint-sized cuffed pants. How many bears do you know
who are this cool, man!

Step by Step

MATERIALS

- ✓ Black fabric (for the body)
- ✓ White fabric (for the arms and sweater; knits preferred)
- ✓ Two dark brown buttons (for the eyes)
- ✓ Tan fabric (for the nose)
- ✓ Brown thread (for the mouth)
- ✓ Stuffing

✶ Patterns: page 135

I love turtlenecks.

Instructions for Beatnik Bear

1. Trace the pattern on the wrong side of the fabric. Leave a ¼" (0.5 cm) seam allowance on all pieces and cut the fabric.

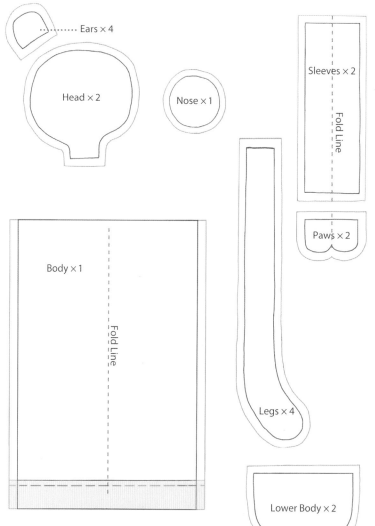

Ears × 4

Head × 2

Nose × 1

Sleeves × 2

Fold Line

Body × 1

Fold Line

Paws × 2

Legs × 4

Lower Body × 2

✶Fabric for the body should measure 8⅝" × 7" (22 × 18 cm). The body can be cut from a sleeve or from any suitable scrap cloth.

2. With right sides of the ear pieces facing, sew the ear along the dotted line (as shown). Turn ears right side out.

3. Sandwich the finished ears into the head pieces, aligning the ear base with the head top. The right sides of the head pieces should be facing. Sew the head along the dotted line (as shown). Turn the head right side out and fill with stuffing through the slit (at the neck).

slit

4. Sew the buttons to the face as eyes. Use a cross stitch through each button's four holes. Make the nose (see below) and attach it to the face. With split running stitches, outline the mouth.

With slip stitches, sew the nose to the face.

With running stitches, sew around the edge of the nose piece.

Tug the stitches gently to create a pouch and fill with small amount of stuffing.

Pull the stitches taut and sew the opening closed.

5. Fold the body fabric, right sides facing. Sew along one side to form a tube, leaving a ¼" (0.5 cm) seam allowance.

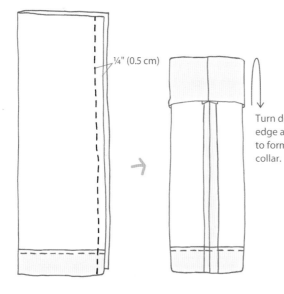

¼" (0.5 cm)

Turn down the top edge about 2" (4.5 cm) to form the turtleneck collar.

6. With a running stitch, sew a circle about 1⅜" (4 cm) down from the collar edge. Pull the thread taut. Fold the collar down about ⅞" (2 cm), stitch along the bottom of the collar to become a hem. Fill in stuffing from the bottom opening of the body part.

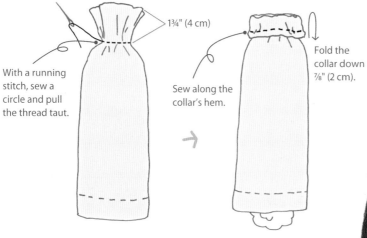

With a running stitch, sew a circle and pull the thread taut.

1¾" (4 cm)

Sew along the collar's hem.

Fold the collar down ⅞" (2 cm).

Stay cool, man.

7. Sew the arm and paw pieces together. Fold them so the right sides are facing, then sew along the edge (as shown). Turn the arms right side out and fill with stuffing.

With a slip stitch, sew the neck inside the collar.

With a slip stitch, sew the arms to the body.

Leave a ¼" (0.5 cm) seam allowance.

8. Working on the wrong side of the fabric, sew the leg pieces together. Turn them right side out and fill with stuffing. Sandwich the legs between the lower body pieces. The right sides of the lower body pieces should be facing. Sew along the edges (as shown). Turn the lower body right side out and fill with stuffing.

With a slip stitch, sew the lower body to the bottom of the sweater.

Note: Only fill the bottom two-thirds of the legs with stuffing.

How to Make the Pants

MATERIALS
- ✓ Dark green corduroy fabric
- ✓ Dark brown thread

★ Patterns: page 135

Instructions

1. Trace the pattern on the wrong side of the fabric. Cut out pattern pieces, leaving seam allowances as shown below.

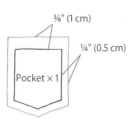

⅜" (1 cm)
¼" (0.5 cm)
Pocket × 1

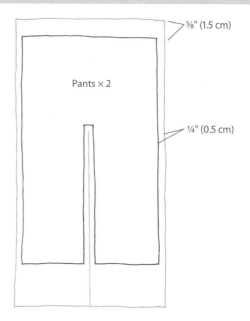

⅝" (1.5 cm)
Pants × 2
¼" (0.5 cm)

2. Sew the pocket (as shown), then sew it to the right side of one pants piece.

From the wrong side of the pocket piece, turn the right side down to create a ⅜" (1 cm) hem. With a running stitch, sew along the edges (as shown), ⅛" (0.2 cm) from the edge.

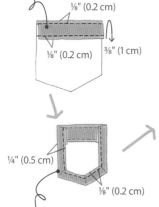

⅛" (0.2 cm)
⅛" (0.2 cm)   ⅜" (1 cm)
¼" (0.5 cm)
⅛" (0.2 cm)

Fold in the sides of the pocket and sew a ¼" (0.5 cm) hem. The stitches along the bottom of the pocket should be ⅛" (0.2 cm) from the edge.

3. With right sides of the pants pieces facing, sew along the outer and inner edges. After sewing the inseam, make a Y-shaped cut in the seam allowance. (The bottom ⅝" (1.5 cm) of each pant leg will form the cuffs.)

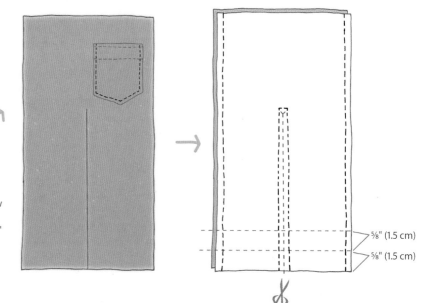

⅝" (1.5 cm)
⅝" (1.5 cm)

4. Pull the pants onto the doll. Fold the waistline inside the pants about ⅝" (1.5 cm) and sew around the waist with a running stitch. Pull the thread gently until the waistline is snug against the body. Double-fold the bottom of the pant legs to make the cuffs.

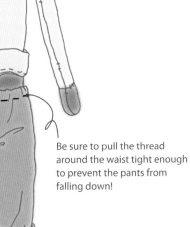

Be sure to pull the thread around the waist tight enough to prevent the pants from falling down!

Each cuff is ⅝" (1.5 cm) wide and double-folded.

The hills are alive!

Prairie Pup

My dog has a split personality. When she drinks from her bowl, there is more water splashed around it on the floor than in her tummy. When she sleeps, her legs are stretched out every which way, and I cannot help but think how graceless she is!

However, when she sits quietly to watch the world go by, she delicately crosses her front legs, and she seems perfectly prim and proper. She has the potential for such elegant posture that I had to model this pup after her.

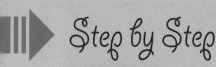

Step by Step

MATERIALS

- ✓ Blue striped sock (for the sweater)
- ✓ Sturdy woven brown fabric (for the head and ears)
- ✓ Striped cotton fabric (for the arms)
- ✓ Light brown fabric (for the paws and legs)
- ✓ Black fabric (for the nose)
- ✓ Red buttons × 2 (for the shoulders)
- ✓ Black thread (for the eyes)
- ✓ Stuffing

★ Pattern: page 136

Dancing dogs are here again.

Instructions for Prarie Pup

1. Trace the patterns on the wrong side of the fabric. Leave a ¼" (0.5 cm) seam allowance.

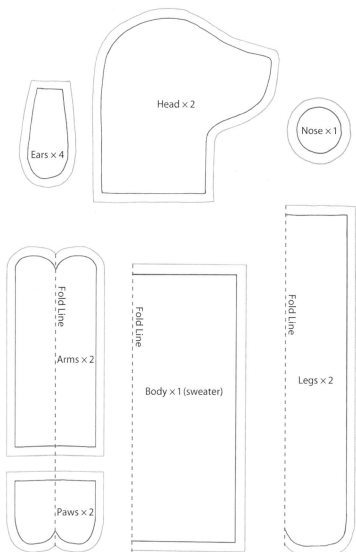

2. With the right sides of the head pieces facing, sew them together (as shown). Turn the head right side out and fill with stuffing through the slit at the neck.

4. With black thread, outline the eyes (as detailed in illustration below). Make a nose with a little bit of stuffing inside, then sew it onto the face.

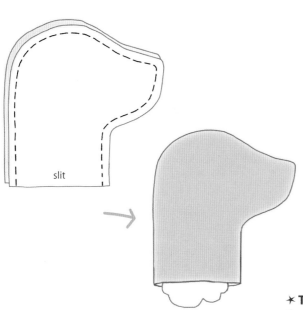

slit

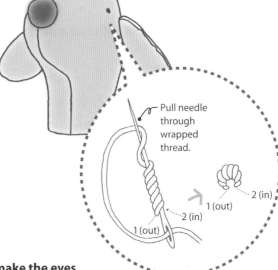

Pull needle through wrapped thread.

1 (out)

2 (in)

2 (in)

1 (out)

3. With the rights sides of the ear pieces facing, sew them together. Turn them right side out. At the opening, fold in a ¼" (0.5 cm) seam. With a slip stitch, sew one ear onto each side of the head.

✶ To make the eyes (bullion stitch): After sewing

the nose, run the needle beneath the fabric and pull the needle out where one of the eyes will be. Wrap the thread around the needle 5–6 times, then pull the needle through while pushing down the loops with your fingers.

Insert the needle at the base of the knot and pull the needle out where the other eye will be. Repeat the bullion-stitch knot. Pull the needle through the nose and make a small secure knot that can be easily hidden.

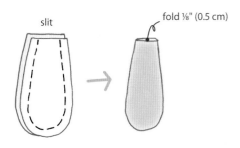

slit

fold ⅛" (0.5 cm)

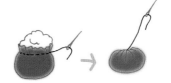

A lot of stuffing will make a round nose, and just a little stuffing will make a flat nose.

5. Fold the leg piece in half vertically, right sides facing, then sew the edges together. Leave the top open. Turn the leg right side out and fill with stuffing.

open

⅞" (2 cm)

Do not fill the top 1" (about 2 cm) with stuffing.

knee area

Pull the sewing thread tighter so the leg curves slightly.

6. Sew the arms and paws together at the straight edge (to create the arms). Fold the whole arm piece in half vertically, right sides together. Sew along the edges of the arm, leaving a ⅞" (2 cm) slit in the middle of the side. Turn the arm right side out and fill with stuffing through the silt.

⅞" (2 cm)

slit

elbow area

Pull the sewing thread tighter so the arm curves slightly.

Tips: To give the dog truly elegant posture, pulling the thread taut at the knees and elbows to create a curve is key. Also, when assembling the body, the slip stitches should be oriented toward the body, not parallel to it. Woof!

7. Cut a 6½" (16 cm) cuff from the striped sock. With the wrong side of the sock out and with a backstitch, sew across the bottom and up one side of the cuff to form a tube that is 3¼" (8 cm) wide. Trim the extra material, leaving a ¼" (0.5 cm) seam allowance.

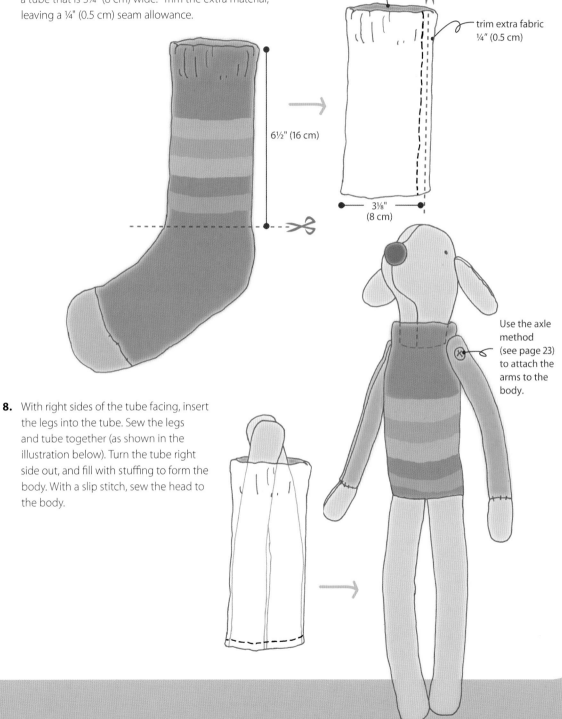

collar

trim extra fabric
¼" (0.5 cm)

6½" (16 cm)

3⅛"
(8 cm)

Use the axle method (see page 23) to attach the arms to the body.

8. With right sides of the tube facing, insert the legs into the tube. Sew the legs and tube together (as shown in the illustration below). Turn the tube right side out, and fill with stuffing to form the body. With a slip stitch, sew the head to the body.

Step by Step

Instructions for the Skirt

1. Draw the outline of the finished skirt on the wrong side of the fabric. Leave ¼" (0.5 cm) and ⅞" (2 cm) seam allowances (as shown below).

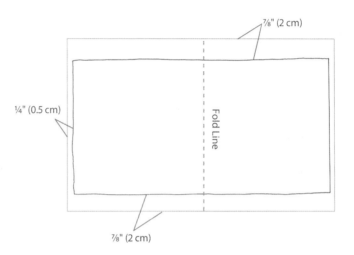

⅞" (2 cm)

¼" (0.5 cm)

Fold Line

⅞" (2 cm)

2. Fold the right side of the fabric to meet the left side, then sew along the left edge. The top opening will be the waist and the bottom opening will be the hem.

Fold the top hem down three times to form a ⅜" (1 cm) wide casing for the elastic waistband. Leave a ⅝" (1.5 cm) slit through which to thread the elastic band.

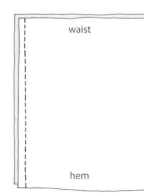

waist

hem

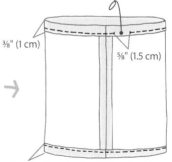

⅜" (1 cm)

⅝" (1.5 cm)

Bottom hem is also ⅜" (1 cm) wide.

3. Attach a safety pin to one end of the elastic band and pull it through the casing. When the ends of the elastic band meet, adjust the waistband to the right diameter for the waist. Sew the ends of the elastic band and trim the excess.

⅜" (1 cm)

For a sturdy waistband, overlap the ends of the elastic band by about ⅜" (1 cm) before sewing them.

Tips: If you leave the slit open in the waistband casing, you can later remove the elastic band when it becomes worn out and needs replacing.

★ Threading the elastic waistband with a safety pin is much easier than tugging and pulling the band through the casing by hand.

Hound Dog

Hound Dog is one of the first dolls I made. The original construction of the doll is fairly simple. Essentially, just sew two pieces of fabric together and fill with stuffing.

Later on, I started to add more clothing to the doll. I finally settled on a pair of worn-out trousers with a small floral pattern and a wool hat.

Step by Step

MATERIALS

- ✓ Red striped fabric
  (for the body)
- ✓ Red wool or other sturdy fabric
  (for the head and paws)
- ✓ Floral fabric (for the arms)
- ✓ Brown patterned fabric
  (for the pants)
- ✓ Black fabric (for the shoes)
- ✓ 2 black beads (for the eyes)
- ✓ Large black button
  (for the nose)
- ✓ Black thread
  (for the whiskers)
- ✓ Stuffing

★ Pattern: page 137

Instructions for Hound Dog

1. Trace the patterns onto the wrong side of the fabric.
    Leave a ¼" (0.5 cm) seam allowance.

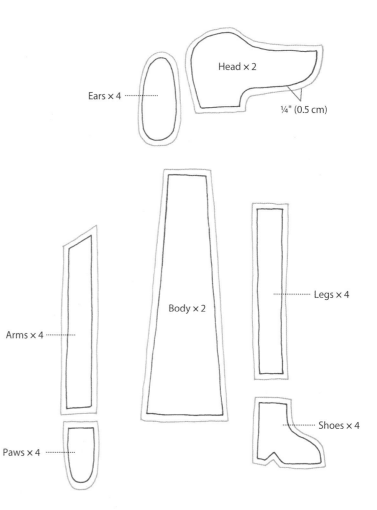

Ears × 4

Head × 2

¼" (0.5 cm)

Arms × 4

Body × 2

Legs × 4

Paws × 4

Shoes × 4

2. With the right sides of the head pieces facing, sew the head. Leave the neck open. Turn the head right side out and fill with stuffing through the slit.

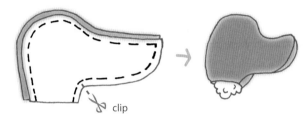

clip

3. With the right sides of the ear pieces facing, sew the ears. Turn the ears right side out. With a slip stitch, sew the ears to the head.

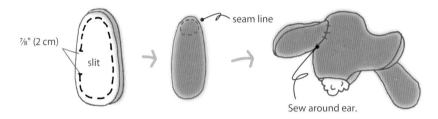

⅞" (2 cm)

slit

seam line

Sew around ear.

4. Sew the small black beads as the eyes. Sew the large black button as the nose. The whiskers are created from knots and doubled-thread stitches.

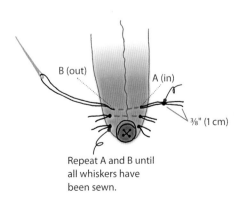

B (out)

A (in)

⅜" (1 cm)

Repeat A and B until all whiskers have been sewn.

A: Tie a knot in the doubled thread and leave a ⅜" (1 cm) tail for the whiskers.
B: Pull the needle out from the other side. Tie another knot close to the fabric. Tighten the knot, leaving another ⅜" (1 cm) tail for the whiskers. Cut the thread.

5. Sew together the paws and arms pieces. Sew the shoe and leg pieces together. With right sides facing, sew the pieces together along the edges (as shown), leaving the arm and leg tops open. Clip the fabric at the bottom of the shoe piece to create a heel. Sew around the clip to shape the heel. Turn the arms and legs right side out and fill with stuffing.

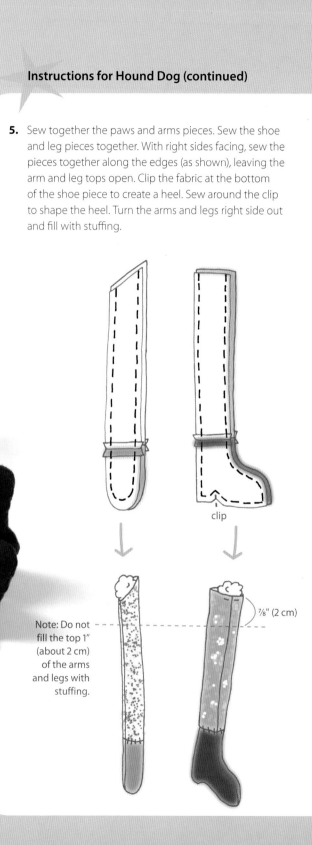

clip

⅞" (2 cm)

Note: Do not fill the top 1" (about 2 cm) of the arms and legs with stuffing.

6. Sandwich the stuffed legs between the body pieces, right sides facing. Sew the pieces together along the edges (as shown). Leave a 1" (2.5 cm) opening on both sides for the arms (as shown). Turn the body right side out through the neck opening and fill with stuffing.

7. With a slip stitch, attach the head to the neck and attach the arms to the body.

Neck opening

1" (2.5 cm)
Arm opening

1" (2.5 cm)
Arm opening

Slip-stitch arm to body

When shaping the heel, do not clip closer than ⅛" (0.2 cm) to the stitches. This will prevent the stuffing from poking through the stitches.

Pants

MATERIALS

✓ Brown patterned fabric
✓ 1 button

★ Pattern: page 137

Instructions

1. Trace the pants pattern on the wrong side of the fabric. Leave the following seam allowances: ⅛" (0.5 cm) on the side and ⅜" (1 cm) on the top and bottom. Remember to cut through four layers of fabric at once, creating two pairs of pattern pieces.

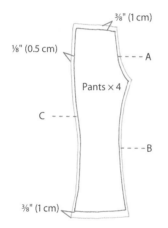

⅜" (1 cm)

⅛" (0.5 cm) — — — A

Pants × 4

C — — —

— — — B

⅜" (1 cm)

2. With the right sides facing, take the first pair of pattern pieces, sew along line A (as shown) and open the fabric. Then repeat this step with the second pair of fabric pieces.

— — — A

3. Face the right sides of the two halves. With a running stitch, sew along B and C (as shown). Turn the pants right side out.

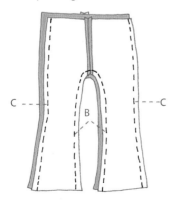

C — — — — — — —C

B

4. Fold a ⅜" (1 cm) cuff on each leg. Fold the waist ⅜" (1 cm) to form the waistband. Sew the decorative button to the front center waistband.

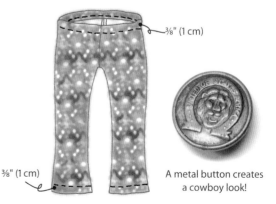

⅜" (1 cm)

⅜" (1 cm)

A metal button creates a cowboy look!

Hat

MATERIALS

✓ 1 knit sock
✓ Thread (to match sock)

Instructions

1. Cut off a section of the sock, about 2½" (6 cm) from the toe.

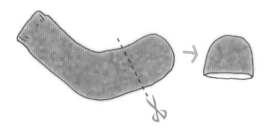

2. With the wrong side of the sock out, fold a ⅞" (2 cm) hem. With a running stitch, sew along the edge of the hem and tighten the stitches slightly to form a brim. Turn the hat right side out.

⅞" (2 cm)

3. To shape the crown: with a running stitch sew along the edge, leaving ⅛" (0.3 cm) from the top.

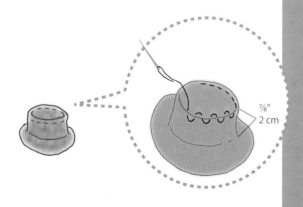

⅞"
2 cm

Doll Story Fun

Cowboy detective is on a mission today . . .

The target: Top of the cliff 300 feet up, where the gang is gathered.

Great—the rope is secure.

(Tummy rumbles)

Only 2 feet from the top . . .

Oh no, I need more fuel!

Now I know I should have eaten breakfast.

Game Over

Long-Legged Fox

I used some material left over from my quilting project to make the long legs of the fox. The colors and patterns of the fabric give this fox a relaxed country feel.

Step by Step

MATERIALS

✓ Green fabric (for the upper body)
✓ Blue fabric (for the body bottom)
✓ Brown fabric (for the face and shoes)
✓ Cream-colored fabric (for the ears and head)
✓ Black fabric (for the back of the ears)
✓ Stripes (for the arms)
✓ Quilt blocks or patchwork fabric (for the legs)
✓ 2 brown buttons (for the shoulders)
✓ 2 gray /white buttons (for the eyes)
✓ 1 black button (for the nose)
✓ Black thread (for the whiskers)
✓ Stuffing

★ Patterns: page 138

Instructions for Long-Legged Fox

1. Trace all patterns onto the wrong side of the fabric. Leave a ¼" (0.5 cm) seam allowance on all pieces.

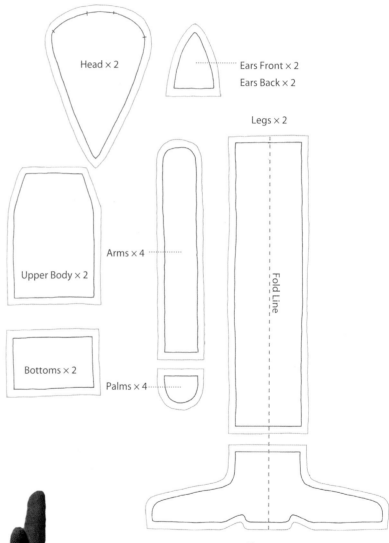

Head × 2

Ears Front × 2
Ears Back × 2

Legs × 2

Arms × 4

Fold Line

Upper Body × 2

Bottoms × 2

Palms × 4

Shoes × 2

2. With right sides of the ear fabric facing, use a running stitch to sew along the tracing lines (as shown). Leave the bottom open, then turn the pieces right side out.

3. Sandwich the two ear pieces between the head pieces, making sure the wrong side of the head pieces are facing out. Sew along the tracing lines of the head pieces (as shown). Leave a ¾" (2 cm) slit.

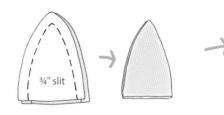

¾" slit

¾" (2cm)

4. Turn the head right side out and fill with stuffing. With a slip stitch, sew the opening closed. Sew on the buttons for the eyes and the nose. Add whiskers (see page 77).

It's time for my close-up.

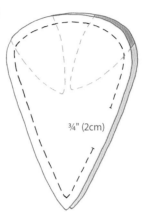

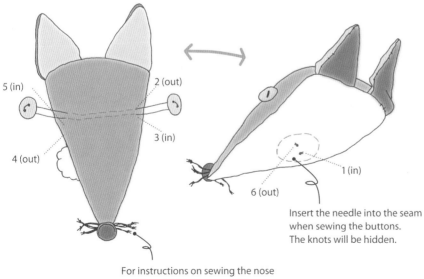

5 (in)

2 (out)

3 (in)

4 (out)

6 (out)

1 (in)

Insert the needle into the seam when sewing the buttons. The knots will be hidden.

For instructions on sewing the nose and the whiskers, see page 77.

5. With wrong sides of the quilt blocks together, sew one quilt block to another until they are the desired length for the legs. On the right side, sew along the seams to create a visible, textural detail.

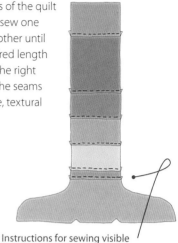

Instructions for sewing visible seams are on page 90.

6. Fold the patchwork leg piece vertically in the middle. With a running stitch, sew the opening at the front of the leg closed. Sew a curved seam near the back end of the shoes to form a heel. Clip into the seam allowances. Turn the leg right side out and fill with stuffing. Leave ¾" (2 cm) at the top without stuffing.

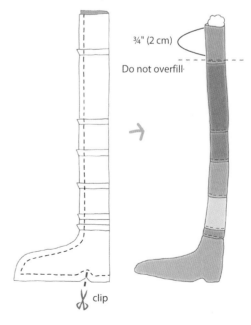

¾" (2 cm)

Do not overfill.

clip

7. Sew the upper body and the body bottom together. Insert the stuffed legs from the neck opening through to the body bottom. With the right sides of the body and bottom pieces together, sew along the tracing line. The top part of the legs will be stitched together with the body bottom (as shown). Turn the body right side out and fill with stuffing.

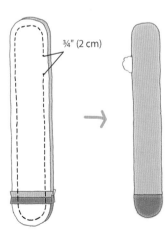

First, sew the upper body to the body bottom.

8. Sew the arm and palm fabric together. Fold the two pieces of fabric, right sides facing. Sew along the tracing line as shown, leaving a ¾" (2 cm) slit. Turn the arm right side out, then fill the arm with stuffing through the slit. With a slip stitch, sew the slit closed.

¾" (2 cm)

9. Sew the arms to the body, using the axle method (page 23). Sew the head to the neck.

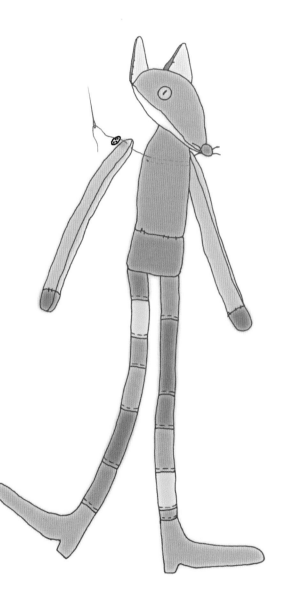

87

Step by Step

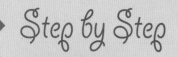

MATERIALS

✓ White fabric
✓ Elastic waistband, 12" (30 cm) long

★ Patterns: page 138

Pants for the Fox

1. Trace the pattern onto the wrong side of the fabric. Leave seam allowances: ¾" (2 cm) on the top and bottom, ¼" (0.5 cm) on the sides.

2. With right sides of the pants fabric together, sew along the traced line. Cut the legs apart following the Y-shaped cutting diagram below. Top and bottom seam allowance: Fold the fabric back once to form a tunnel around ½" (1 cm) wide and leave a ¾" (1.5 cm) opening on the back (for the elastic band).

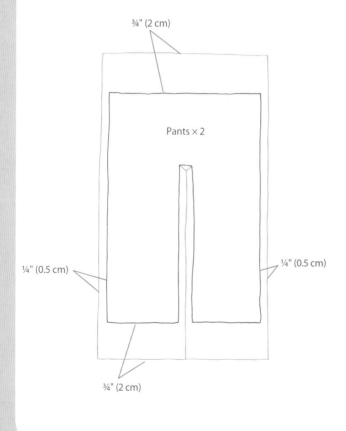

¾" (2 cm)

Pants × 2

¼" (0.5 cm)

¼" (0.5 cm)

¾" (2 cm)

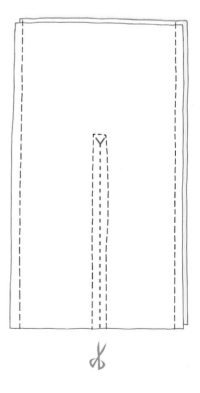

3. At the top and bottom seam allowances, fold the fabric to the wrong side to form a tube about ⅜" (1 cm) wide. Sew along the seamline (as shown). Leave a ¾" (2 cm) opening in the top seam for inserting the elastic waistband.

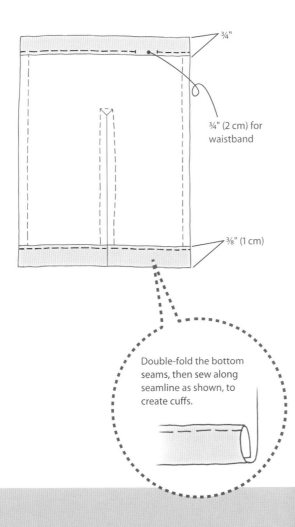

¾"

¾" (2 cm) for waistband

⅜" (1 cm)

Double-fold the bottom seams, then sew along seamline as shown, to create cuffs.

The only part Billy is missing is his legs. We are almost there . . .

"It is such a waste to throw out all these little pieces. I will attach them together like I'm quilting!"

"Always more and more to recycle . . ., can't waste a thing . . ."

"I do not want such long legs, no . . . . !!"

Bonus Technique

SIMPLE QUILTING

All sewers have lots of leftover fabric from different projects. Finding clever ways to recycle these leftovers is an ongoing challenge.

Quilting is an ideal way to reuse these leftover fabrics. Assembling scraps into quilt blocks or patchwork fabric is like playing with puzzle pieces. Every way you arrange the pieces offers a new combination of color and texture. You can even sew several little pieces into a single, long length of fabric without a plan in mind. Quilt blocks can be sewn by hand or with a sewing machine.

Before sewing leftover pieces, try to cut them into similar shapes and sizes, and cut their edges square. Arrange them in different combinations to determine your design before you sew.

Quilting Instructions

1. With the right sides of two pieces together, sew one side seam.

2. Open the fabric so the right side is facing out. You can sew a running stitch along the seam to highlight it.

3. Repeat steps 1 and 2 with additional fabric pieces. The running stitches on the right side give the patchwork a handmade feel. Machine sewing will give it a neater look.

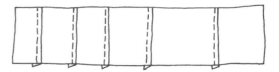

90

Blue-toned palette

Red-toned palette

Floral-patterned palette

Contrasting palette

Sleepy Beagle

This pooch has one body but expresses two
different states of being: dreaming (on one side
of the face) and awake (on the other side). Use
this clever decorative technique to create other
opposing expressions: happy and sad, serious
and fun, and so on.

Step by Step

MATERIALS

✓ Green fabric (for the head, arms, legs, and outer ears)

✓ Brown fabric (for the inner ears)

✓ Black fabric (for the nose)

✓ Blue and white fabric (for the body)

✓ 1 black bead (for the pupil)

✓ 1 large brown bead (for the eye)

✓ Dark brown thread (for the mouth and eyes)

✓ Stuffing

★ Patterns: page 140

Instructions for Sleepy Beagle

1. Trace the patterns on the wrong side of the fabric. Leave a ¼" (0.5 cm) seam allowance all around. Cut the fabric.

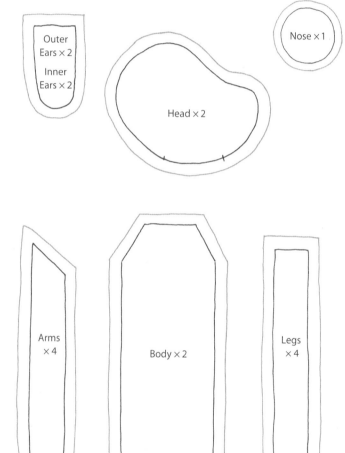

Outer Ears × 2
Inner Ears × 2

Nose × 1

Head × 2

Arms × 4

Body × 2

Legs × 4

2. With the right sides of the fabric together, sew the arms pieces and legs pieces (as shown). Leave the tops open. Turn right side out and fill with stuffing through the opening. Leave ⅞" (2 cm) at the tops without stuffing.

3. Insert the legs and arms into the body fabric (as shown below). Make sure the body pieces' right sides are facing. Sew the body fabric and the arms and legs together (as shown). Turn the body right side out and fill with stuffing through the open neck.

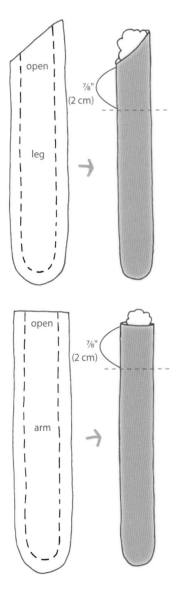

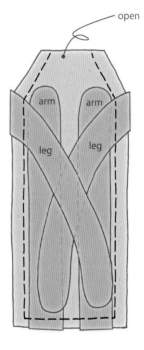

✷ When sewing the parts together, be sure to sew only along the black seamline, and do not catch any arms or legs in the seam! The limbs should move freely.

Good morning!

Instructions for Sleepy Beagle (continued)

4. With right sides facing, sew the head pieces together. Leave a ⅞" (2 cm) slit at the bottom. Turn the head right side out and fill with stuffing.

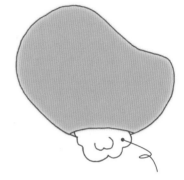

⅞" (2 cm)

With a slip stitch, sew the slit closed after stuffing.

5. With right sides facing, sew one inner ear piece to one outer ear piece (as shown). Turn right side out and sew the opening closed. Repeat for the other ear. With a slip stitch, sew both ears to the head.

Slip-stitch the ears and nose to the head.

Sew the opening closed.

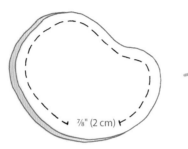

6. With a running stitch, sew around the edge of the nose piece. Pull the thread taut to form a pouch. Fill the pouch with stuffing, then pull the thread tight to close the opening. Sew the nose to the head.

Good night!

7. With a threaded sewing needle and beads, sew the two different facial expressions (as shown below). Thread the smaller bead on top of the larger one as shown to form the "awake" eye.

Sew the head to the neck.

Clothing and Accessories

MATERIALS

- ✓ Striped fabric, 4" × 12" (10 × 30 cm) (for the skirt)
- ✓ White lace, 1" × 4¼" (1.5 × 12 cm) (for the sash)
- ✓ 1 clear button and 1 pink button (for the belt)
- ✓ Assorted small beads (for the necklace)
- ✓ 3 purple buttons (for the top)

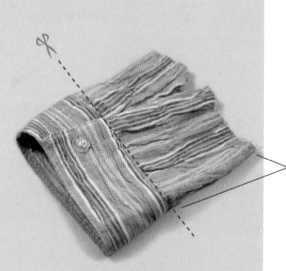

✶ I used part of a sleeve for the skirt fabric. Cut a 4" (10 cm) length from the sleeve. The sleeve's width will most likely be a good fit for the skirt.

Instructions

1. Fold the fabric in half lengthwise so the right sides of the fabric are facing. Sew the fabric together ¼" (0.5 cm) from the edge.

¼" (0.5 cm)

2. Fold the skirt hem, ⅜" (0.7 cm) wide. Fold it inward three times. Sew along the hem ⅛" (0.2 cm) away from the edge.

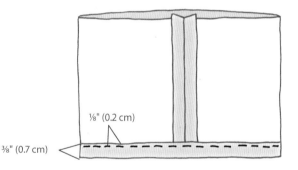

4" (10 cm)

⅛" (0.2 cm)

⅜" (0.7 cm)

3. After making the skirt pleats (see below), put the skirt on the doll. Cinch the waistline thread to adjust the waist size. Sew the skirt onto the body.

✶ With a running stitch, sew along the waistline. Pull the thread gently to make pleats.

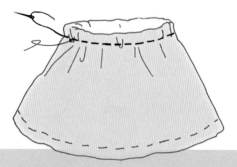

4. For each side of the body, use different accessories to give them distinct looks.

String the beads together with a thin needle and thread to make a necklace.

Sew the lace sash around the waistband. Where the lace ends meet, sew the clear button.

Sew the three small purple buttons along the center of the top, spaced 7/8" (2 cm) apart.

Sew the pink button to the opposite side of the sash.

Flexible Frog

For most of the previous projects, only two pieces of fabric were used to make the body of the doll. This is an easy way to sew the dolls, but it also limits their shape and structure.

Introducing a few new pattern pieces to the basic construction gives the doll a three-dimensional figure. To add this layer of structure, you need to take extra measurements and calculate the fabric size more carefully. You can practice these techniques with the Flexible Frog.

Step by Step

MATERIALS

✓ Horizontal-striped fabric
(for body sections A and C)
✓ Vertical-striped fabric
(for body sections B and D)
✓ Checkered fabric
(for the body back)
✓ Green fabric (for the head back)
✓ Green floral-print fabric
(for the forehead)
✓ Olive fabric (for the mouth
and arms)
✓ Gray fabric (for the sleeves)
✓ Floral-print fabric (for the legs)
✓ Cream-colored fabric
(for the shoes)
✓ Brown fabric (for the soles)
✓ 2 dark brown buttons
(for the shoulders)
✓ 2 white buttons (for the eyes)
✓ Light green thread (for the mouth)
✓ Maroon thread (for the eyes
and eyelashes)
✓ Stuffing

★ Patterns: page 141

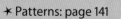

My legs are
really long!

Instructions for Flexible Frog

1. Trace the patterns on the wrong side of the fabric.
Leave a ¼" (0.5 cm) seam allowance. Cut the fabric.

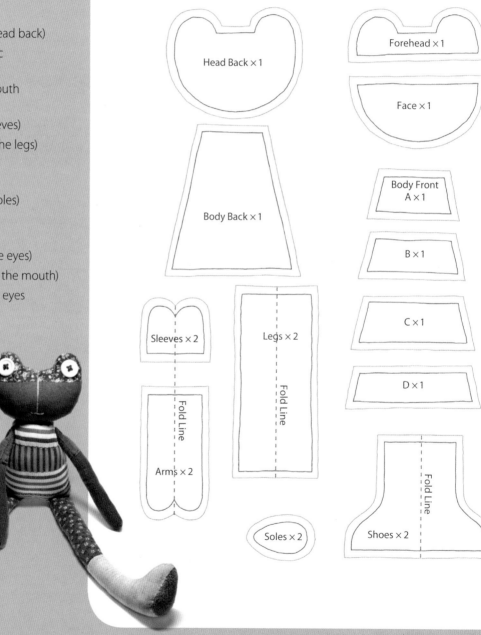

Peekaboo!

2. Sew together the forehead and the face fabrics first. Then sew the front and back of the fabric for the face together. Make sure the right sides of the fabric are facing.

Clip the seam allowance at the top of the head to shape the ears. Leave a ¾" (2 cm) slit for the neck.

¾" (2 cm)

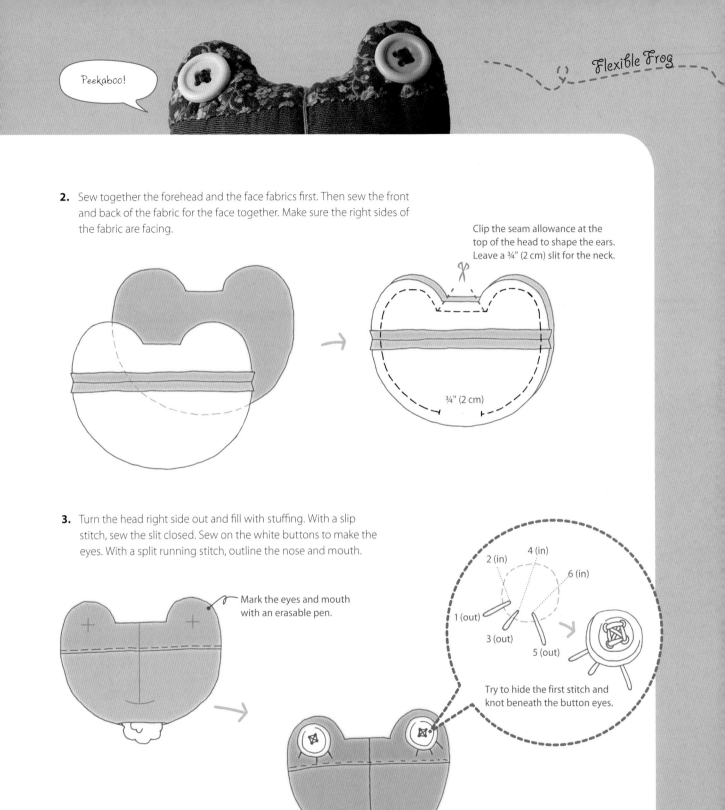

3. Turn the head right side out and fill with stuffing. With a slip stitch, sew the slit closed. Sew on the white buttons to make the eyes. With a split running stitch, outline the nose and mouth.

Mark the eyes and mouth with an erasable pen.

2 (in) 4 (in) 6 (in)

1 (out)

3 (out) 5 (out)

Try to hide the first stitch and knot beneath the button eyes.

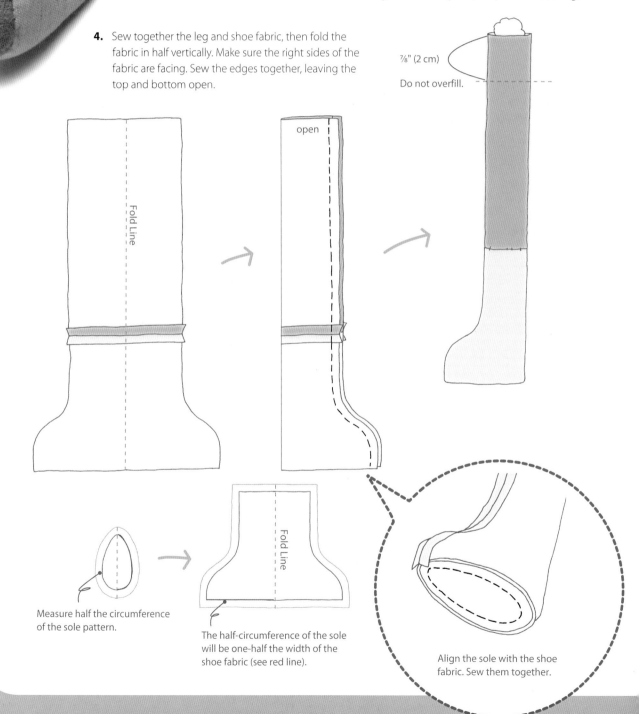

5. From the wrong side of the fabric, sew together the shoe and the sole fabric. Turn the leg right side out and fill with stuffing. Leave the top ⅞" (2 cm) without stuffing.

4. Sew together the leg and shoe fabric, then fold the fabric in half vertically. Make sure the right sides of the fabric are facing. Sew the edges together, leaving the top and bottom open.

⅞" (2 cm)

Do not overfill.

open

Fold Line

Fold Line

Measure half the circumference of the sole pattern.

The half-circumference of the sole will be one-half the width of the shoe fabric (see red line).

Align the sole with the shoe fabric. Sew them together.

6. Sew body front fabric sections A, B, C, and D together. With right sides of the body front and body back fabrics facing, sew the edges (as shown).

7. Sandwich the stuffed legs in the body (as shown). Sew them together along the top of the legs.

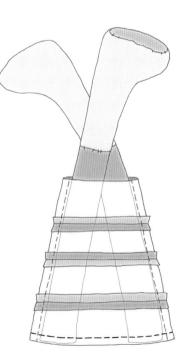

8. Turn the body right side out. Fill the body with stuffing.

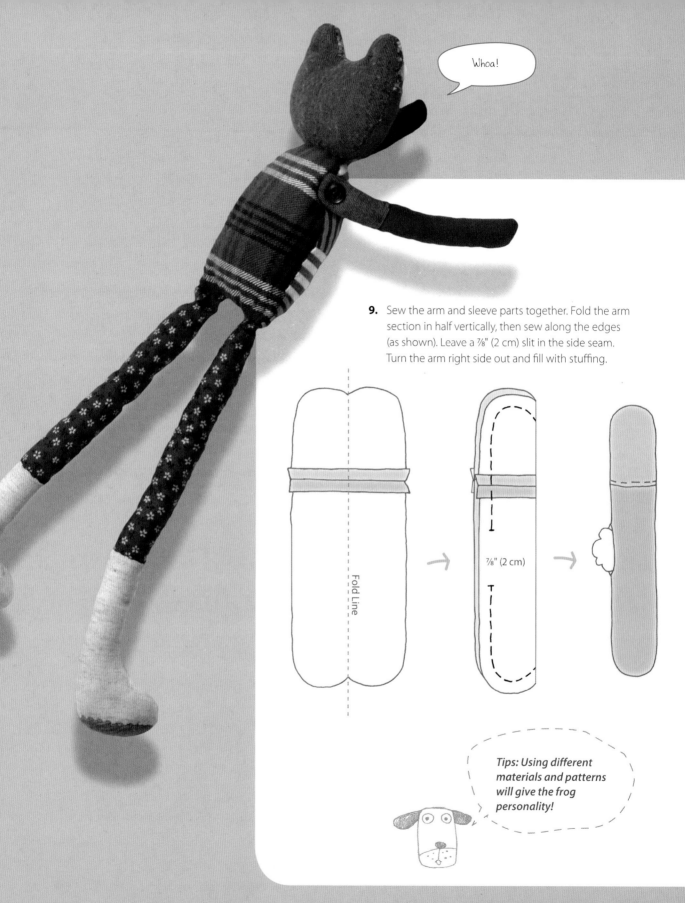

Whoa!

9. Sew the arm and sleeve parts together. Fold the arm section in half vertically, then sew along the edges (as shown). Leave a ⅞" (2 cm) slit in the side seam. Turn the arm right side out and fill with stuffing.

Fold Line

⅞" (2 cm)

Tips: Using different materials and patterns will give the frog personality!

10. With a slip stitch, sew the head to the body. Using the axle method (see page 23) and two buttons, sew the arms to the body.

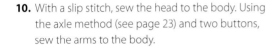
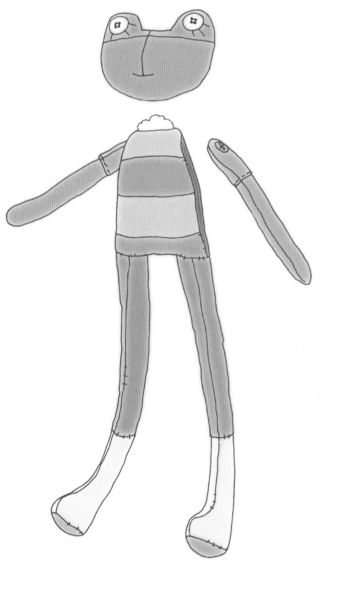

Lotus pose: Cross the legs and start to breathe deeply. You can relax and meditate in this position.

Shoulder stand: Roll onto your back and extend your legs over and behind your head. This will rejuvenate your whole body!

Try to place your legs behind your shoulders and head. This is a bit advanced. You need a lot of flexibility. You ask, "Are there any yoga tricks I can't do?"

Let me lie down and think about that.

"Ommm . . . mmmmmm . . . ."

Popo Piggy

Dressing your dolls in the right clothes is the best way to express their personalities. If you do not want to make separate clothes for your dolls, you can pre-plan and incorporate clothing into the doll's body when you make it. This little piggy's T-shirt is part of its body!

The inspiration for this doll came when I found the large cream-colored button. I thought it would be perfect for the snout of a pig. From that one object, the rest of the design came naturally.

Step by Step

MATERIALS

✓ Light brown fabric
   (for the head, arms, outer ears, and
   nose; durable fabrics such as hemp
   or corduroy preferred)

✓ Light-colored patterned fabric
   (for the inner ears)

✓ Black fabric (for the hooves)

✓ Pink, blue, and white striped fabric
   (for the shirt)

✓ Green fabric (for the pants)

✓ 2 small light blue beads
   (for the pupils)

✓ 2 dark blue flat buttons
   (for the eyes)

✓ 1 large cream-colored button
   (for the snout)

✓ Maroon thread (for the mouth)

✓ Stuffing

★ Patterns: page 142

Instructions for Popo Piggy

1. Trace the patterns onto the wrong side of the fabric (as shown). Leave a ¼" (0.5 cm) seam allowance on all pieces. Cut the fabric.

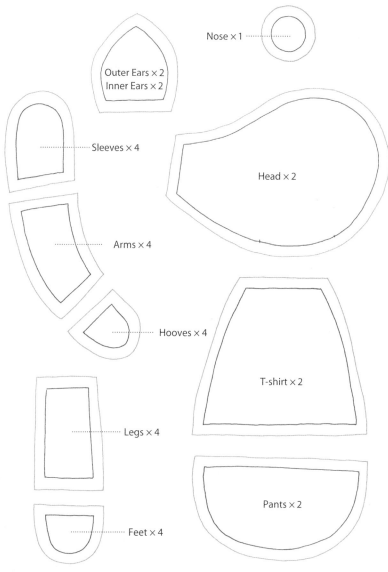

Nose × 1

Outer Ears × 2
Inner Ears × 2

Sleeves × 4

Head × 2

Arms × 4

Hooves × 4

T-shirt × 2

Legs × 4

Pants × 2

Feet × 4

I like mud pies.

2. With right sides facing, sew the head pieces together (as shown). Leave a ¾" (2 cm) slit at the neck.

¼" (0.5 cm)

¾" (2 cm)

To make the snout, sew the round nose piece to the front of the face (as shown). Turn the head right side out and fill with stuffing.

3. With the maroon thread, outline the mouth (see details below). Each eye is a combination of the small bead (as the pupil) and the large bead. Sew the large cream-colored button to the front of the nose to complete the snout.

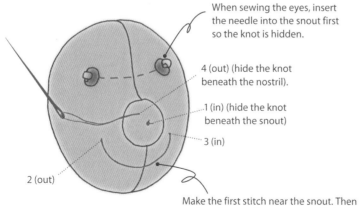

When sewing the eyes, insert the needle into the snout first so the knot is hidden.

4 (out) (hide the knot beneath the nostril).

1 (in) (hide the knot beneath the snout)

3 (in)

2 (out)

Make the first stitch near the snout. Then outline the mouth. Be sure to pull the thread taut when sewing the mouth so it has a firm shape and will sink into the skin slightly.

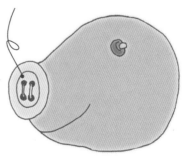

Sew two parallel lines across the button holes to highlight the pig's nostrils.

4. With right sides facing, sew the sleeve, arm, and hoof pieces together. Leave a 7⁄8" (2 cm) slit on the side of the arm. Sew the leg and foot pieces together. Sew the T-shirt and the pants pieces together, leaving the top open.

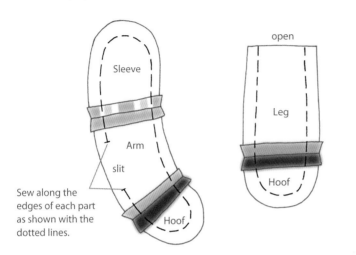

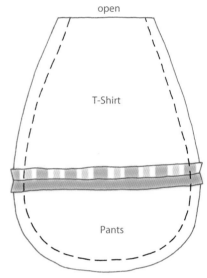

Sew along the edges of each part as shown with the dotted lines.

5. Turn each section right side out. Fill each piece with stuffing.

Use an awl to push the stuffing into corners and other hard-to-reach places!

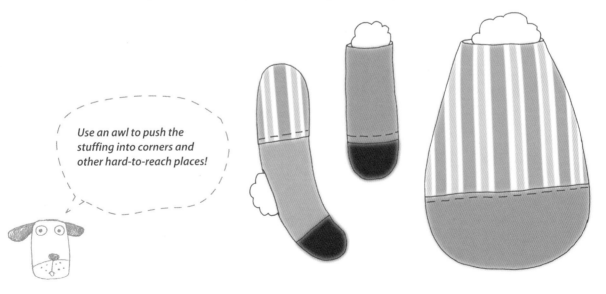

6. With right sides facing, sew the ear pieces together. Turn the ears right side out. With a slip stitch, sew the opening closed.

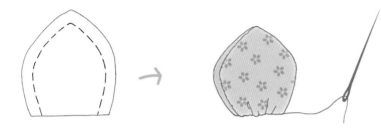

7. With a slip stitch, sew the head to the body. Position the patterned inner ears so they face forward, then sew the ears to each side of the head. Also use a slip stitch to sew the legs to the body.

Ear placement

Use the axle method (see page 23) and two buttons to sew the arms to the body.

For strong and sturdy legs, densely pack the legs with stuffing. If the legs are strong, the pig can be propped upright against a wall.

Leg placement

Mr. Wiggles

Craft wires are available in most craft stores. These wires have many uses in doll making. Aside from shaping a wiggly worm, they can help give shape to a doll's body. They can give support to dolls designed to sit or stand upright. Also, the wires can form the core shape of special doll parts or accessories.

Step by Step

MATERIALS

✓ Green furry fabric, such as
  a towel (for the body)
✓ 2 craft wires
  (for the armature/skeleton)
✓ 2 small black beads (for the pupils)
✓ 2 round orange beads and
  2 flat white buttons (for the eyes)
✓ Stuffing

★ Patterns: page 139

Instructions for Mr. Wiggles

1. Trace the patterns onto the wrong side of the fabric. Leave a ¼"
   (0.5 cm) seam allowance. Cut the fabric.

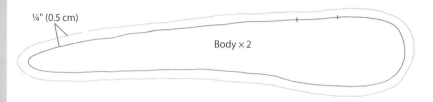

¼" (0.5 cm)

Body × 2

2. With right sides together, sew the body pieces together. Leave a ⅞" (2 cm) slit
   in the side seam. Turn the body right side out.

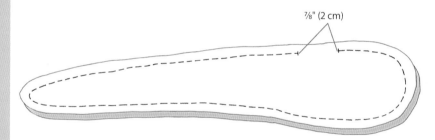

⅞" (2 cm)

3. Fill the body from the tail end and work toward the head. Try to spread
   the stuffing as evenly as possible to give the whole body a smooth look.
   Create the eyes by stacking the two beads on top of the button. Sew
   the eyes to the head.

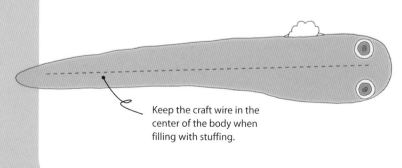

Keep the craft wire in the
center of the body when
filling with stuffing.

Tape the sharp ends of craft wires to protect your fingers.

✳ To give the worm a stronger-shaped body, use two craft wires twisted together. Tape one end and insert it into the body. Fill the body with stuffing. Cut the extra wire through the slit and tape the sharp end before sewing the slit closed.

Worms love rice!

I ♥ books

Worms that like computers are usually called viruses.

Spotlight

SHAPING WITH CRAFT WIRES

Craft wires can be used in several ways in doll making including to form the armature of the body and to shape different doll parts. The wires are easily twisted and molded so many variations are possible.

Consider taping the sharp ends of the wires before using them in dolls, especially if the dolls will be handled by children. Covering the sharp ends will prevent the wires from puncturing the skin.

Shaping the Wires

1. Use one or two wires depending on how strong you want the armature to be. Twist two wires together or fold one wire in half. Cut the wire(s) to the desired length.

Ideas for Using Craft Wires

1. Monkey arms and tail

Cut craft wire to the desired length and tape the sharp ends.

Push the wire through the finished fabric for the arms.

Use the above (basic) method to insert the wire into the arms or double the wire to create a curved tail.

2. Rabbit ears

Cut the craft wire to the desired length and tape the sharp ends.

Create a U shape and insert it into the ear.

With a running stitch, sew the wire in position along the ear. Shape the wire into an upright rabbit ear.

1. Craft wires used in the monkey's arms and tail.

2. Craft wires used in the rabbit ears.

Appendix

Playing Dress Up

Many projects in this book include their own clothing patterns. Here are a few more tips, techniques, and pieces to inspire you.

Recycled clothing imparts a lot of character and originality on the new dolls that wear them. Miya's A-line skirt is made from a denim scrap and trimmed with lace. Sven's hat is sewn from a piece of a sock, and the scarf is snipped from an old sweater. Uma's dress is from the sleeve of a printed cotton shirt.

Uma

Sven

Miya

Scarf

MATERIALS

✓ Knit fabric from a sweater, any color

Instructions for Scarf for Sven

1. Cut a piece of knit fabric from an old sweater that measures about 8" × 2" (20 × 5 cm).

Fold Line

2. With right sides facing, fold the fabric in half. Leaving a ¼" (0.5 cm) seam allowance, backstitch the long edges together.

¼" (0.5 cm)

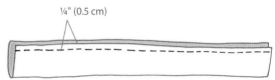

3. Turn the scarf right side out. Stitch both ends closed, leaving a ⅜" (1 cm) hem on both sides.

⅜" (1 cm)

Loosen the knit loops with a needle or awl to fray and fluff the ends.

Hat

MATERIALS

✓ 1 striped sock

Instructions for Hat for Sven

1. From the cuff of the sock, measure 3¼" (8 cm) along the tube and cut the fabric.

3¼" (8 cm)

2. Orient the cuff at the bottom. The tube will be the top of the hat. With a running stitch, sew a circle around the sock, ¾" (2 cm) from the top.

¾" (2 cm)

Loosen the knit loops with a needle or awl to create a pom-pom topper.

3. Pull the thread taut and tie in a knot. Cut the fabric at the top into ⅜" (1 cm) strips.

⅜" (1 cm)

123

Top

MATERIALS

✓ Purple polka-dot fabric
✓ Thread or ribbon

★ Patterns: page 143

> I ♥ Sven.

Instructions for Top for Miya

1. Trace the pattern on the wrong side of the fabric. Leave ¼" (0.5 cm) and ⅜" (1 cm) seam allowances (as shown at right).

⅜" (1 cm)

¼" (0.5 cm)

Top × 2

Fold Line

⅜" (1 cm)

2. Sew the sides of the body and the shoulders together. Clip underneath the arms. Turn the top right side out.

> *Cotton fabric does not have much elasticity. Make sure the neck opening is large enough to fit around the head before you cut the fabric.*

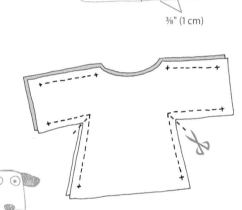

3. Fold the neckline in ¼" (0.5 cm) and sew a hem. Thread a large needle with the thread or ribbon and sew a running stitch along the neckline. Leave the ends long in front. Tie a knot at each end.

4. At the cuffs and bottom hem, fold in the seam allowance three times to conceal the unfinished edges. With a running stitch, sew along the fabric edges.

The thread or ribbon can be adjusted to tighten or loosen the neckline.

¼" (0.5 cm)

A-Line Skirt

MATERIALS

✓ Denim scraps
✓ White lace trim

★ Pattern: page 143

Instructions for Skirt for Miya

1. Select denim scraps for the front and back of the skirt. (Try to use the seam as part of the front design). Trace the patterns onto the denim.

2. Leave seam allowances as shown below. Make sure you place the seam on one side of the shirt on the front, not at the center. Sew the lace trim along the seam.

3. With right sides together, sew the two skirt pieces together. Turn the skirt right side out. Fold in the ⅜" (1 cm) seam allowances at the waist and the bottom hem. Sew both hems.

Using the sturdy machine-stitched seam from the side of the jeans adds built-in structure to the skirt. Add white lace trim along the seam.

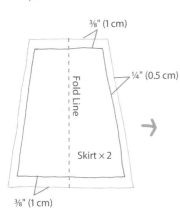

⅜" (1 cm)

¼" (0.5 cm)

Fold Line

Skirt × 2

⅜" (1 cm)

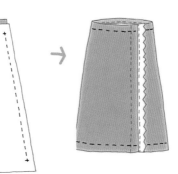

Handbag

MATERIALS

✓ Knit fabric or felt, 3⅛" × 5½" (8 × 14 cm)
✓ Rope, yarn, or cord (for the handles)

1. Trace and cut the fabric. With right sides together, sew the bag body together.

2. At the bag opening, fold the fabric down ⅜" (1 cm) and sew along the seamline. Turn the bag right side out.

3. Add a zigzag stitch trim along the edge of the bag as decoration. Sew the handles at the top of the bag.

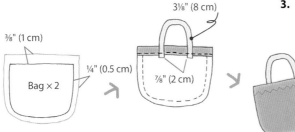

⅜" (1 cm)

¼" (0.5 cm)

3⅛" (8 cm)

⅞" (2 cm)

Bag × 2

Dress

MATERIALS

★ Patterns: page 143

✓ Floral-print fabric, originally from a shirt sleeve
✓ White lace
✓ Buttons

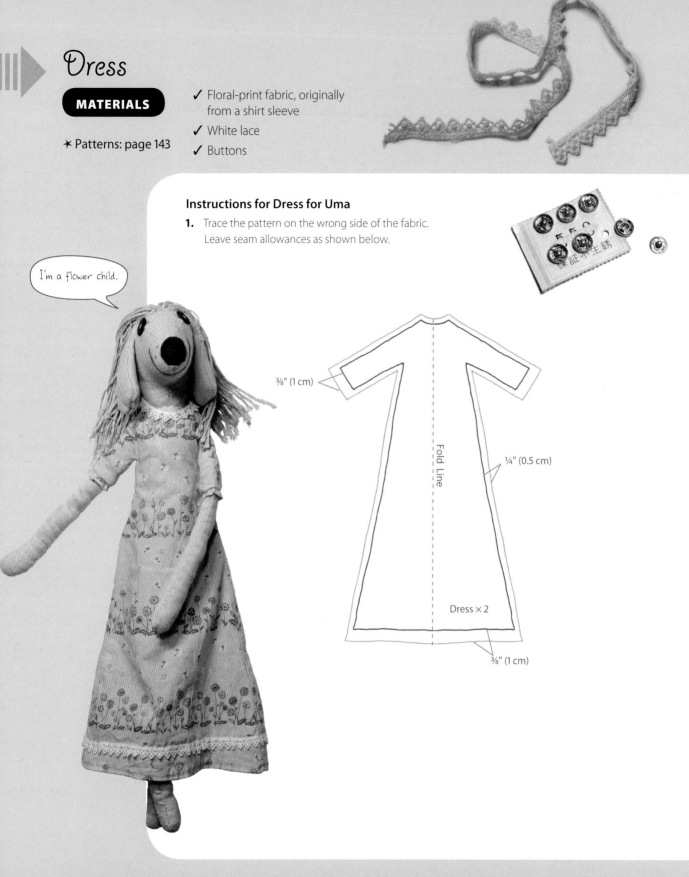

I'm a flower child.

Instructions for Dress for Uma

1. Trace the pattern on the wrong side of the fabric. Leave seam allowances as shown below.

⅜" (1 cm)

¼" (0.5 cm)

Fold Line

Dress × 2

⅜" (1 cm)

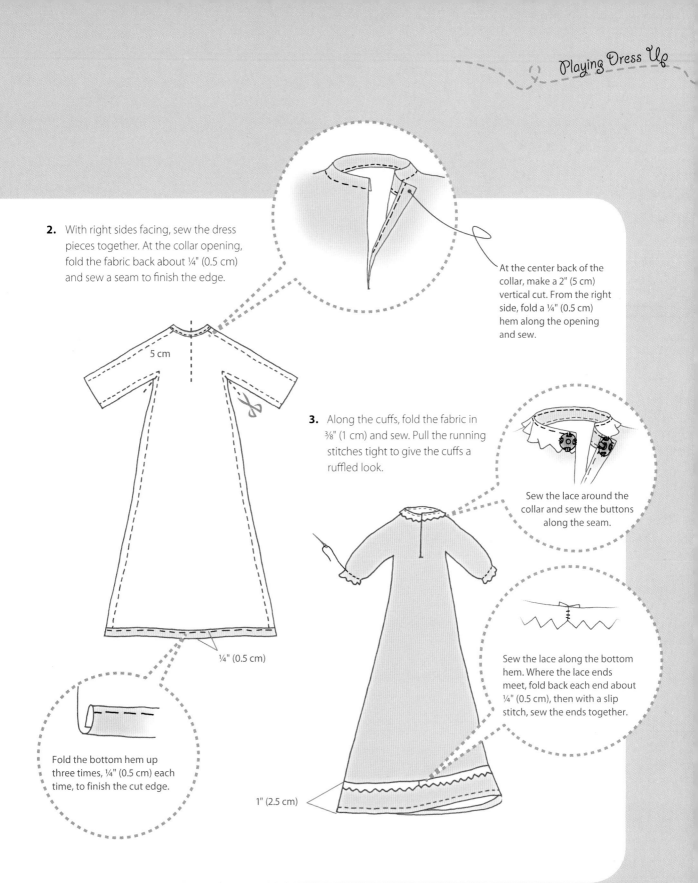

2. With right sides facing, sew the dress pieces together. At the collar opening, fold the fabric back about ¼" (0.5 cm) and sew a seam to finish the edge.

At the center back of the collar, make a 2" (5 cm) vertical cut. From the right side, fold a ¼" (0.5 cm) hem along the opening and sew.

5 cm

3. Along the cuffs, fold the fabric in ⅜" (1 cm) and sew. Pull the running stitches tight to give the cuffs a ruffled look.

Sew the lace around the collar and sew the buttons along the seam.

¼" (0.5 cm)

Sew the lace along the bottom hem. Where the lace ends meet, fold back each end about ¼" (0.5 cm), then with a slip stitch, sew the ends together.

Fold the bottom hem up three times, ¼" (0.5 cm) each time, to finish the cut edge.

1" (2.5 cm)

Pattern Notes

* All patterns are printed at 100% (actual size) except for the clothes on page 143. These patterns can be enlarged or reduced to fit the size of your doll.

* The dotted lines show where to place the pattern on the fold when tracing or cutting fabric.

* The black lines are the finished pattern outlines. Always add a standard seam allowance (¼" or 0.5 cm) around the pattern when cutting the fabric unless instructed otherwise.

* To preserve the pages of this book, trace the pattern pieces onto tracing paper or tissue. You can also photocopy the pattern pages.

* Due to the space restrictions of the page, some patterns overlap. These patterns can also be photocopied or traced.

* Some of the doll projects do not have patterns in the book. For these projects, refer to the project instructions for drawing your own patterns.

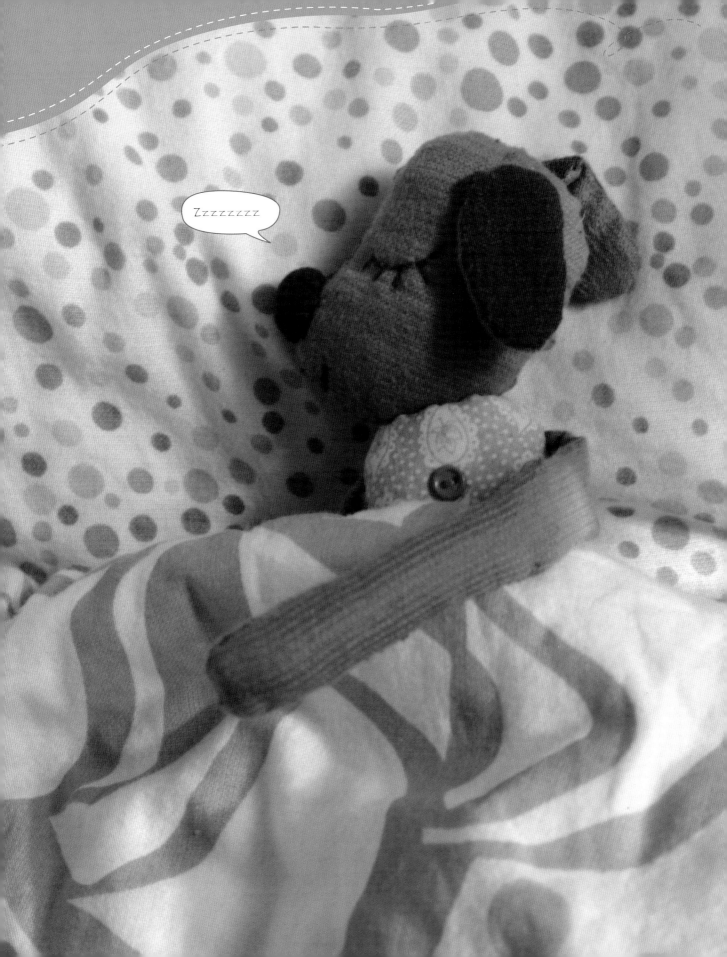

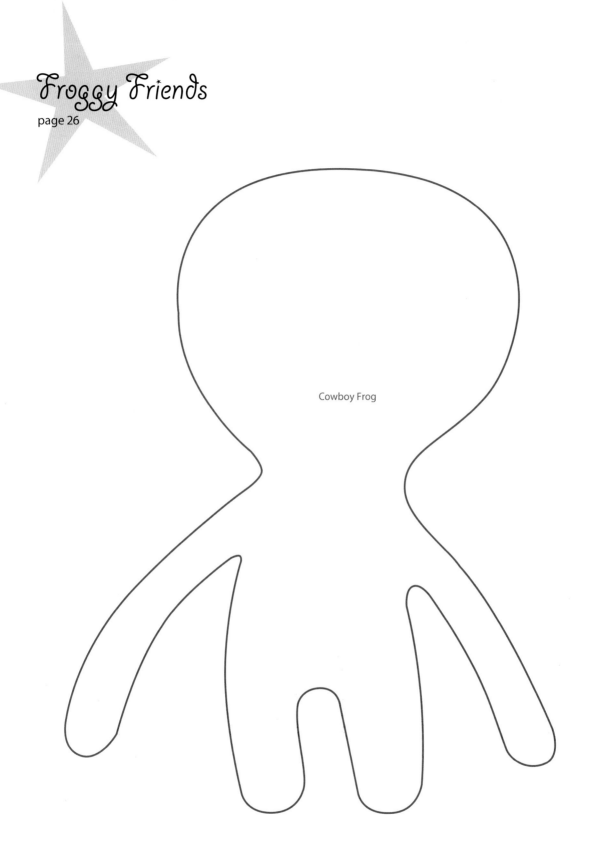

Cowboy Frog

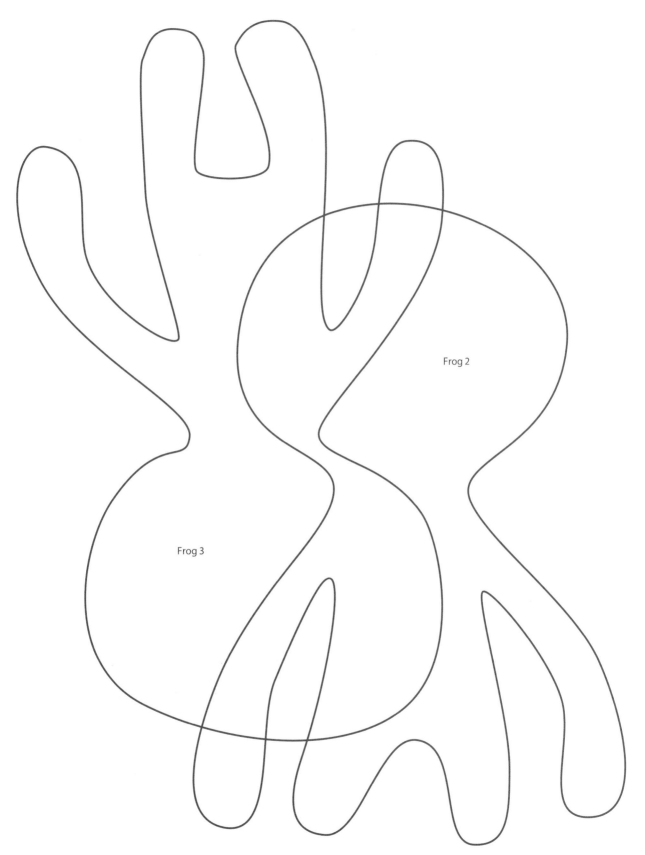

Frog 2

Frog 3

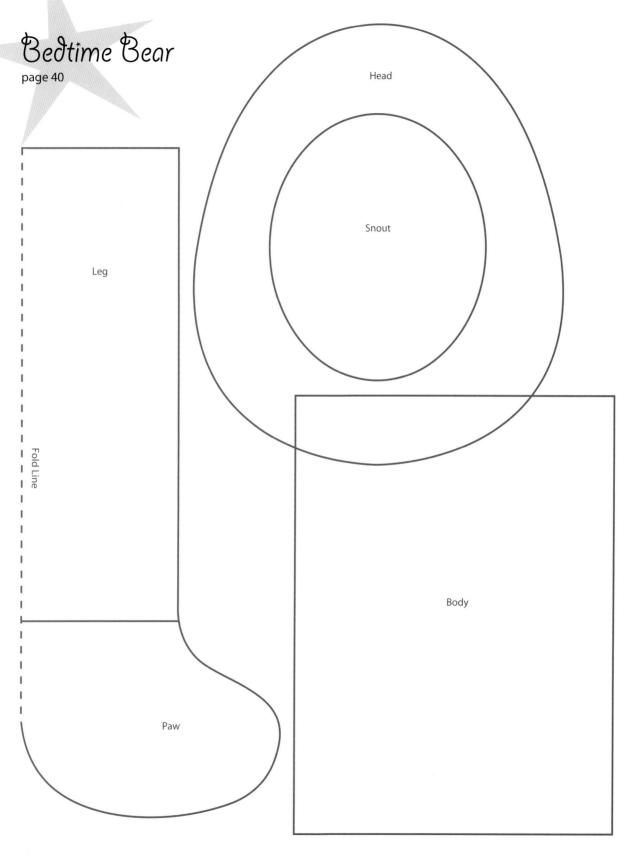

Bedtime Bear

page 40

Head

Snout

Leg

Fold Line

Paw

Body

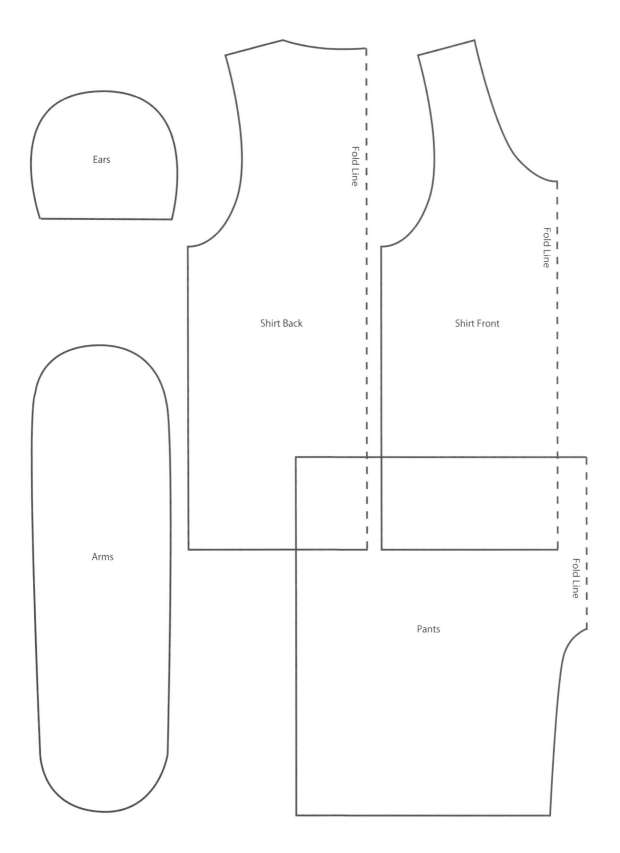

Ears

Shirt Back

Fold Line

Shirt Front

Fold Line

Arms

Pants

Fold Line

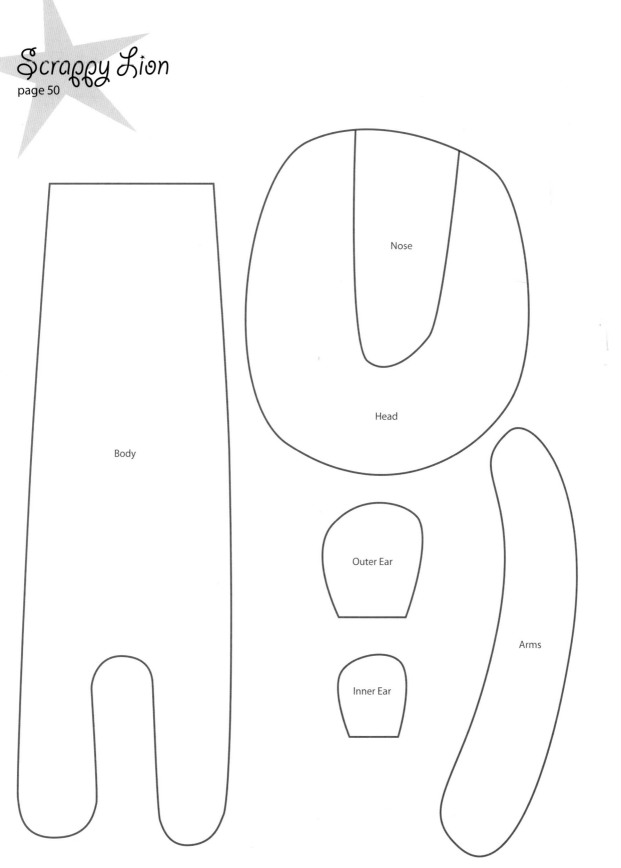

Scrappy Lion
page 50

Body

Nose

Head

Outer Ear

Inner Ear

Arms

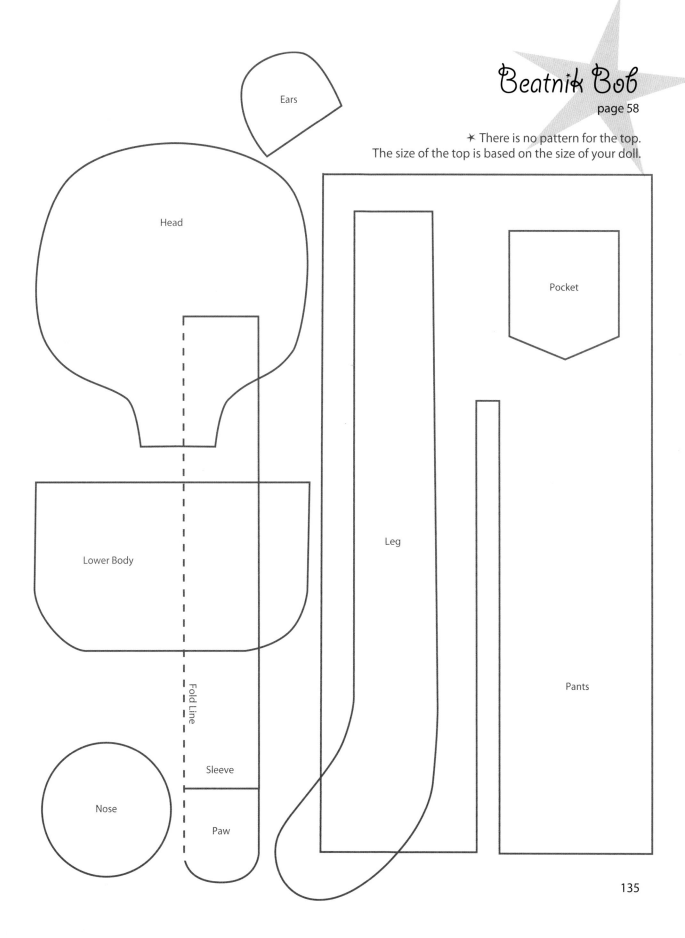

Ears

Beatnik Bob
page 58

★ There is no pattern for the top.
The size of the top is based on the size of your doll.

Head

Pocket

Lower Body

Leg

Pants

Fold Line

Sleeve

Nose

Paw

Prairie Pup

page 66

★ There is no pattern for the skirt. Refer to the project instructions for cutting the fabric.

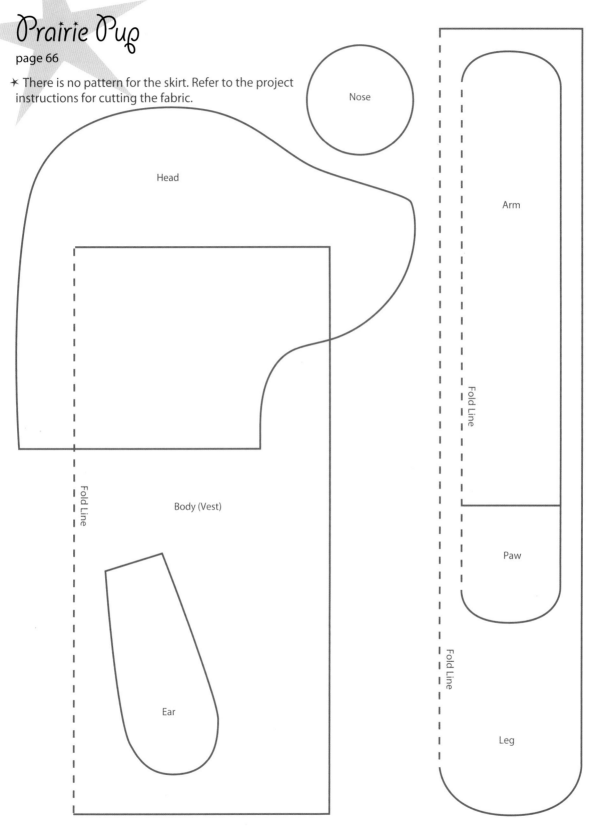

Nose

Head

Arm

Fold Line

Body (Vest)

Fold Line

Paw

Ear

Fold Line

Leg

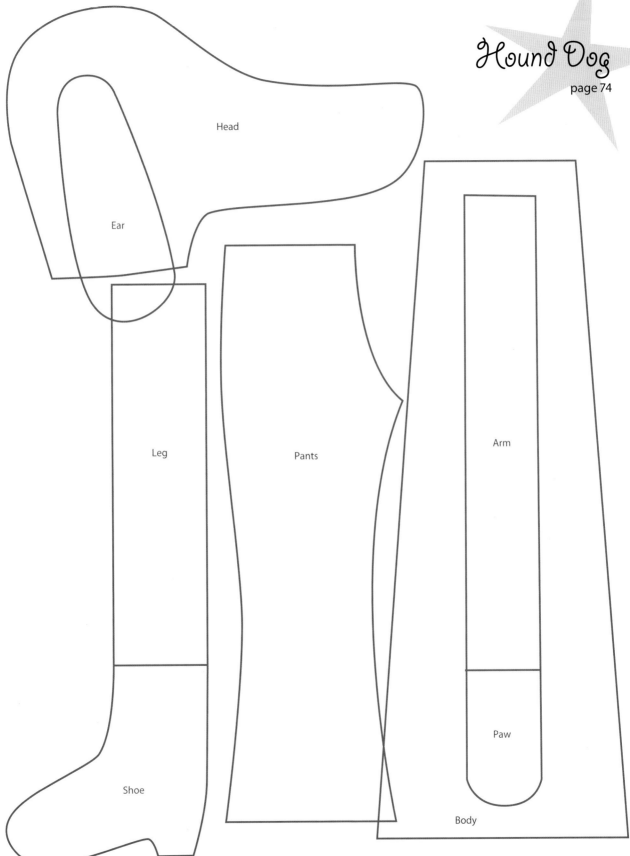

Hound Dog
page 74

Head

Ear

Leg

Pants

Arm

Shoe

Paw

Body

137

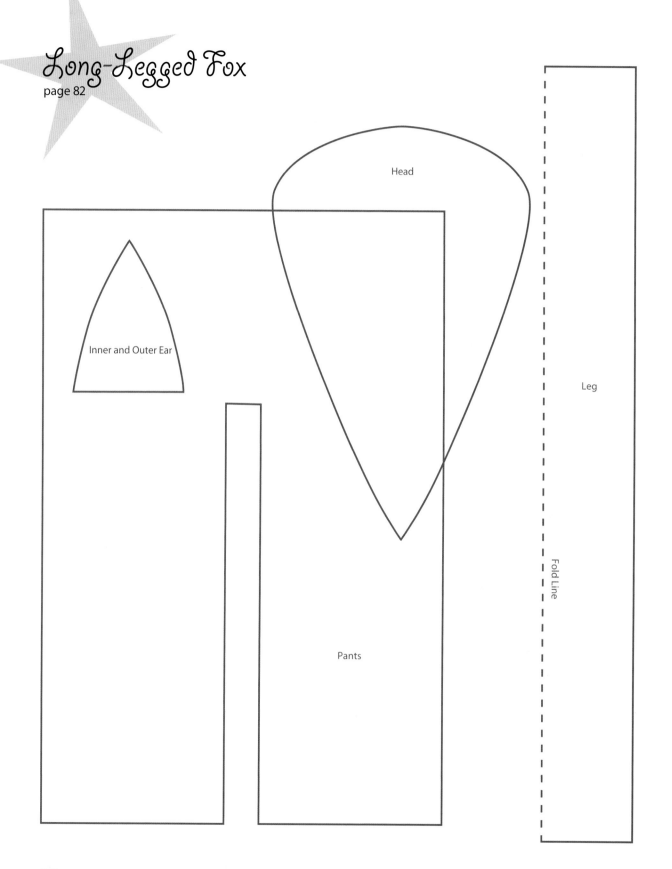

Head

Inner and Outer Ear

Leg

Fold Line

Pants

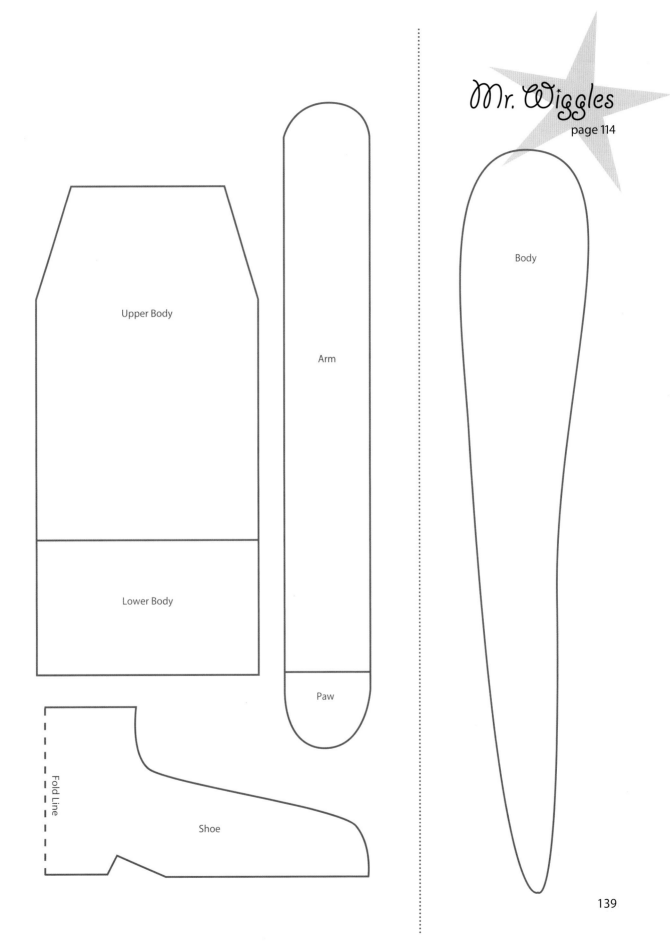

Upper Body

Lower Body

Arm

Paw

Fold Line

Shoe

Mr. Wiggles
page 114

Body

139

Sleepy Beagle
page 92

★ There is no pattern for the skirt. Refer to the project instructions for cutting the fabric.

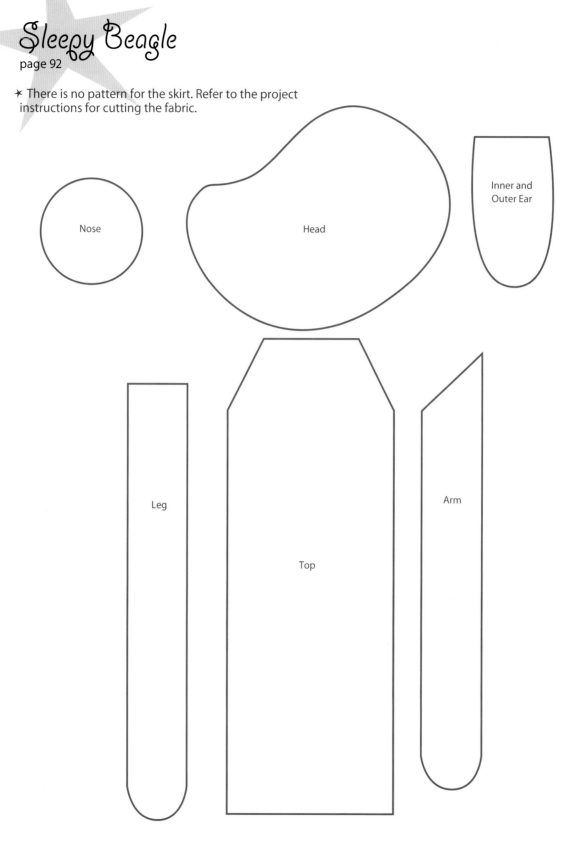

Nose

Head

Inner and Outer Ear

Leg

Top

Arm

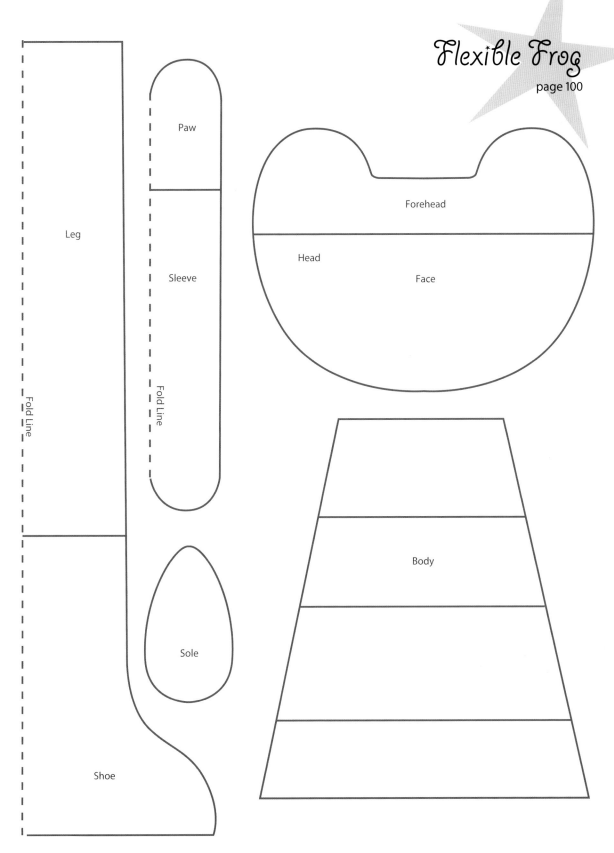

Paw

Leg

Sleeve

Fold Line

Fold Line

Forehead

Head

Face

Sole

Body

Shoe

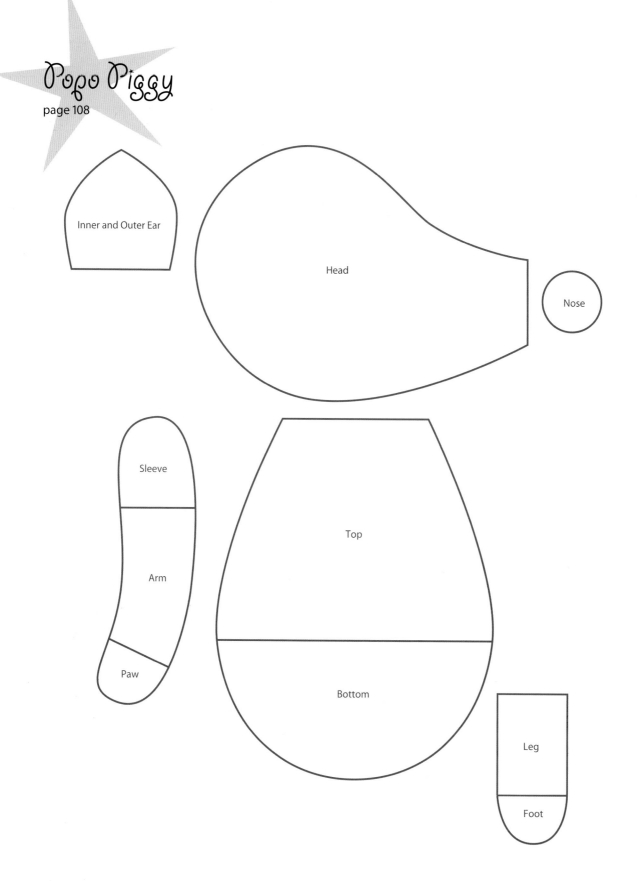

Popo Piggy
page 108

Inner and Outer Ear

Head

Nose

Sleeve

Top

Arm

Paw

Bottom

Leg

Foot

142

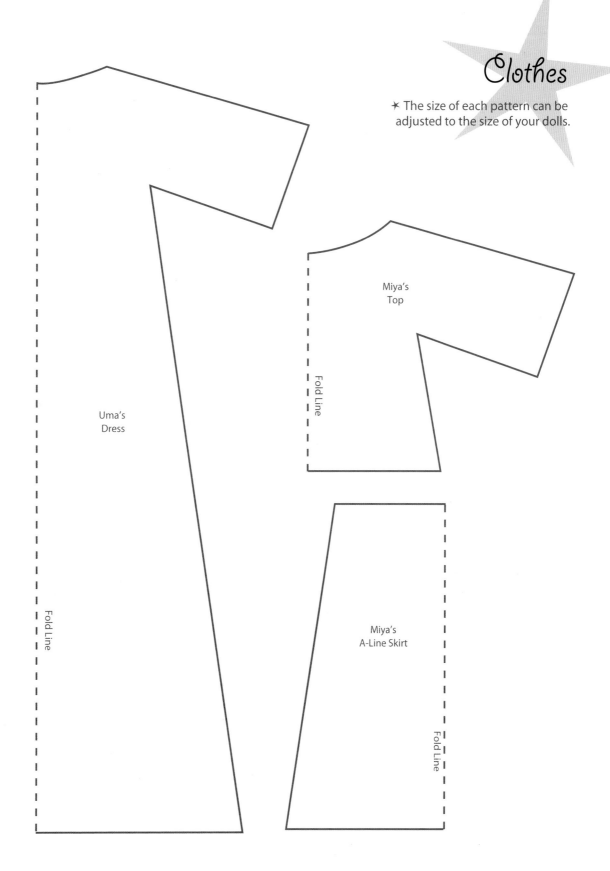

Clothes

★ The size of each pattern can be adjusted to the size of your dolls.

Miya's
Top

Fold Line

Uma's
Dress

Fold Line

Miya's
A-Line Skirt

Fold Line

About the Author

Acknowledgments

Hsiu-Lan Kuei studied fine art in college, and after graduating became a costume designer, home goods designer, and an illustrator.

As a professional costume designer, Hsiu-Lan Kuei has also created puppet and doll characters for stage adaptations of many fairy tales, including *The Ugly Ducking, The Emperor's New Clothes,* and *Snow White.* She lives in Taiwan.

I would like to thank the people who supported me during the creation of this book and who made its publication possible:

The publisher, editors, and designers of Yuan Liou Publishing in Taiwan. From the writing and editing to the design of the book, they have put endless hours into making the book a reality.

In particular I'd like to thank my husband, who shot the photos, helped with the design of the book, and put many months of his spare time to support me while I finished the book. Thank you also to those good friends of ours who lent us their digital camera for shooting, let us use their beautiful homes for some of the photo shoots, and who gave me a lot of valuable advice on clothes-making techniques.

Index